This book is dedicated to eve
spend time in the b
Ignore anyone who dares to h
because they want to use the facilities and get stuck into this book.
Learn fun facts, terrific trivia, and marvelous minutiae.

ISBN Paperback: 978-1-068367007
ISBN Hardcover: 978-1-068367014

For rights and permissions, please contact:

alex@alexsmartbooks.com

BAMSE The Hero Dog

Bamse was a St Bernard dog that became the heroic mascot of the Norwegian navy during the Second World War.

- If a fight broke out on the ship, Bamse would put his paws on the sailors' shoulders and calm them down.

- When a man with a knife attacked a young sailor, it was Bamse who shoved the assailant into the sea and dragged the victim back on board the ship.

- If the ship was taking part in a battle, Bamse wore a special helmet and took up his position on the front gun tower of the boat, boosting the morale of the ship's crew.

- When the sailors went ashore, it was Bamse's job to round them up at the end of the evening and get them safely back to the ship on time. In order to do this, he needed to take a bus, so the crew got him a bus pass which they attached to his collar.

Bamse became very well known, so much so, that he posed for a photo whilst wearing a Norwegian sailor's cap and the photograph was used on Christmas cards.

After the war, Bamse was awarded the PDSA gold medal for devotion to duty and bravery and several statues were erected in his honor.

ENGLISH LANGUAGE

- Rhythms - Longest word without a vowel.
- Go! - Shortest complete sentence.
- Pangram - A sentence that uses every letter in the English language at least once,
  e.g. Amazingly few discotheques provide jukeboxes.
- Pneumonoultramicroscopicsilicovolcanoconiosis - longest word in the dictionary and refers to a lung disease.
- 'I' - shortest word and it is always written as a capital letter.
- There are no perfect rhymes for words like 'orange,' 'month,' 'silver,' and 'purple.'
- Palindromes - words or phrases that are spelled the same both forwards and backward,
  e.g. Was it a car or a cat I saw? A man, a plan, a canal, Panama!.
- Set - the most definitions in the English Language.
- Isogram - a word with no repeating letters e.g. Lumberjack and Uncopyrightable.
- Ambigrams - look the same when turned upside down e.g. NOON.
- Almost - the longest word with its letters in alphabetical order.
- Dictionaries constantly add new words. Recently added words include 'screen-share', 'dirty fries', and 'washi tape'.

Bodacious Bananas

Shine a UV light on a banana and prepare to be wowed as it bursts into a brilliant blue glow! As these fruity wonders ripen, their peels break down chlorophyll into quirky fluorescent catabolites, turning them into the most dazzling bananas in the bunch!

Bananas are technically classified as berries. The banana flower has only one ovary, which develops into a single banana. It also has the structure botanically required of berries—a soft outer skin called the exocarp, a fleshy middle called the mesocarp, and finally, the endocarp, the innermost part containing the seeds.

There's a reason why banana flavor doesn't taste like bananas. Banana flavor comes from the compound isoamyl acetate. Natural bananas have it, and it's the top secret behind every banana-flavored candy. However, banana candies have much more isoamyl acetate than the real deal, which accounts for the taste difference. Banana-flavored candy used to taste exactly like the Gros Michel variety of bananas, which contained plenty of isoamyl acetate. It was the most widespread banana variety until the fungal Panama disease almost wiped it out entirely in the 1960s. Since then, the Cavendish banana has mostly been the variety that we eat today, and this has lower levels of isoamyl acetate, which is why things that are banana-flavored do not taste the same as actual bananas.

Banana do not technically grow on trees. Banana plants are actually giant herbs and are related to ginger.

The third Wednesday in April is World Banana Day.

NIFTY NAMES

NIBLINGS
The gender neutral term used to refer to nieces or nephews.

GEORGE
Originally, the planet Uranus was named after King George III and called Georgium Sidus which is Latin for 'George's star'. This caused arguments amongst astronomers and the planet was renamed Uranus.

NURDLE
A name for the blob of toothpaste that sits on your toothbrush before you start brushing.

TITTLE
The name for the dot that appears in the letter 'i' and 'j'

SPAGHETTO
A single strand of spaghetti.

HOBBLESKIRT
A nickname for the distinctive shape of the Coca Cola bottle. A Hobbleskirt was a fashion trend in the 1910's where the skirt became narrow below the knees and effectively made the wearer hobble.

INTERGLUTEAL CLEFT
Fancy name for your butt crack.

Iceland has a museum dedicated to the penis.
More than 200 penises are on display, most belonging to land and sea mammals found in Iceland.
If you get peckish whilst visiting, the museum has got you covered with a cafe serving savory and sweet penis shaped waffles.

The Museum of Broken Relationships in Croatia offers a way to express heartache and move on from failed relationships.
The exhibits consist of items donated by visitors and include the stories behind the donated items.
Gross Items on display include belly button lint and a 27 year old scab whilst the more poignant items are the number '2' and an iron used to iron a wedding suit.

Osaka, Japan is home to a Cup Noodle museum where visitors can design their own cup noodle flavor combination and enjoy a cookery workshop making chicken ramen.

Massachusetts used be the home of the Museum of Bad Art.
The marketing suggested that good art makes you feel untalented so it's better to look at bad art and feel better about your own skills.

The Avanos Hair Museum consists of a cave filled with 16,000 locks of hair from women from all around the world.
The museum began when a potter's friend was moving away and left the potter a lock of her hair as a memento. After this, every woman who came to the potter's shop and heard the sad story gave him a lock of her hair as well as their contact details.
Twice a year, 10 of the hair samples are picked at random and their owners win a prize. This has, of course, encouraged more women to donate hair and hence the collection has grown.

Weird Museums

Fast Facts

- The world's first flushing toilet was invented by Sir John Harington in 1596, and this is the reason why toilets are nicknamed 'The John'.
- India has a museum dedicated to toilets. It includes different models of toilets, a demonstration of the workings of a cesspit, and models of disguised commodes. The museum entrance is free of charge.
- Rumor has it that Ben Affleck gifted Jennifer Lopez a gem-studded toilet seat worth over $100K. The toilet seat was custom-made and included pearls, rubies, sapphires, and a large diamond. It is thought that JLo can't bear to sit on anything dirty so she takes her special toilet seat with her to be used wherever she is staying.
- France's King Louis XIII had a toilet built into his throne so that he didn't waste any time visiting the bathroom. Instead, he would carry on meetings whilst also using the toilet. His court jester was said to have remarked that, oddly, the King ate his meals in private but defecated in public.
- In Medieval Europe, people used a bucket for an overnight toilet and then threw the waste out of the window in the morning. This led to the invention of stiletto heels so that women could avoid getting their feet in the sewage.
- There was a great deal of human waste on the streets of Europe in 1641, and it needed clearing up! The people came up with a solution. They let pigs loose to roam the streets and eat the waste.
- A US company called Incinolet developed a toilet that uses heat to reduce human waste to ash, so the toilet does not need a septic tank, drainage system, or chemicals. They were originally commissioned by the US Navy to be used on submarines.

- A toilet in Amsterdam actually talks to the users, giving them advice. It's fitted with sensors that enable the intelligent toilet to pass on the appropriate message. A man who used the toilet standing up was given the suggestion that he sat down on the next occasion. Another visitor received an apology from the toilet, stating that the last occupant had not followed the basic rule of hygiene. The toilet also loves to remind users to wash their hands.
- The English King Henry VII had a servant called the Groom of the Stool. His job was assisting the King when he used the toilet, and he may have even been involved in wiping the King's bottom for him. However, the job was considered an honor as the servant had unrestricted access to the Monarch.
- US President Lyndon B. Johnson was famous for insisting that his aides accompany him to the bathroom so that no time was wasted during the working day. He often left the stall door open while he continued conversations.
- Most toilets in the United States flush in the musical key of E flat.
- On average, women take 90 seconds to use a toilet compared to 40 seconds for men.
- The phrase 'spend a penny' originated from the use of coin locks on public toilets in the UK. This practice started in 1850 and continues to this day, as many public restrooms require payment before they can be used.
- A public toilet in China installed a facial recognition system in the bathrooms. Each person scanning their face received a small amount of toilet paper. The aim is to prevent people from using too much paper or stealing it to take home. Once they have scanned their face and received paper, they cannot get any more for seven minutes.
- A toilet snorkel is a long length of flexible tubing designed to pass through a toilet's water trap and access the semi-fresh air from the vent pipe. It's meant to be used if a building is on fire so that the user can breathe fresh air instead of smoke until they are rescued from the building.

Mindblowing Things To Tell Your Friends

A sugar-cube-sized piece of a neutron star would weigh about a billion tons on Earth.

There's a giant water cloud in space surrounding a quasar, holding 140 trillion times the water in Earth's oceans.

A day on Venus is longer than a year on Earth. Venus takes 243 Earth days to rotate once but only 225 Earth days to orbit the Sun.

The sun makes up 99.8% of our solar system's mass with the rest shared among planets and debris.

Jupiter has a giant storm older than modern civilization.
The Great Red Spot on Jupiter has been raging for at least 350 years.

A year on Mercury is just 88 Days. Mercury's orbit around the Sun is so fast that a year is less than three Earth months long.

THE TOWN THAT COULDN'T STOP DANCING

In the summer of 1518, a bizarre phenomenon swept through the streets of Strasbourg in France. Known as the 'Dancing Plague,' this unusual event saw dozens—and eventually hundreds—of people uncontrollably dancing for days on end. The epidemic began in July when a woman named Frau Troffea started dancing fervently in the streets. Within a week, dozens had joined her, and by the end of the month, the number had swelled to hundreds.

The Symptoms and the Spread

Those afflicted with the "plague" reportedly danced until they collapsed from exhaustion. Eyewitness accounts describe the dancers as being in a trance-like state, seemingly unable to stop despite the toll it took on their bodies. Physicians of the time attributed the phenomenon to "hot blood".

Efforts to Cure the Plague

Ironically, city authorities attempted to cure the dancers by encouraging more dancing. They hired musicians and built stages, hoping that the participants would "dance it out" of their systems. Unfortunately, this strategy only exacerbated the situation, leading to a growing public health crisis.

Modern Theories

The Dancing Plague has baffled historians and scientists for centuries. While some believe it was caused by ergot poisoning—a hallucinogenic mold that grows on damp rye—this theory doesn't fully explain the epidemic's contagious nature. Others argue it was a form of mass psychogenic illness, triggered by extreme stress and the pressures of society.

The Legacy of the Dancing Plague

By September 1518, the Dancing Plague had subsided as mysteriously as it began, leaving behind no clear answers. Today, it reminds us of human behavior's strange and sometimes inexplicable nature.

The Dancing Plague of 1518 remains one of history's most curious and chilling mysteries, a surreal chapter that continues to captivate the imagination of scholars and storytellers alike.

FAMOUS WAITERS

Brad Pitt

Before becoming a Hollywood A-lister, Brad Pitt worked as a waiter and even donned a chicken costume to promote a fast-food restaurant. He took on these jobs to support himself while taking acting lessons and auditioning for roles in Los Angeles.

Madonna

Before becoming the Queen of Pop, Madonna worked at Dunkin' Donuts in Times Square. Though she was fired for squirting jelly filling on customers, the job helped her scrape by while she pursued her music dreams.

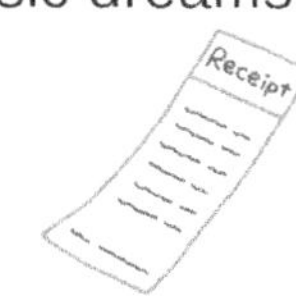

James Franco

While attending UCLA and taking acting classes, James Franco worked the late shift at McDonald's to pay for school. He even practiced accents while taking drive-thru orders, a skill that helped him later in his acting career.

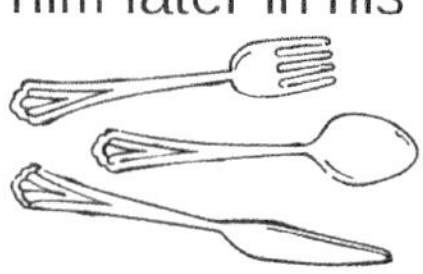

Chris Pratt

Before he became a Marvel superhero, Chris Pratt was working as a waiter at Bubba Gump Shrimp Co. in Hawaii. It was there that a director discovered him and offered him a small role, kickstarting his acting career.

Lady Gaga

As a young woman in New York City, Lady Gaga worked as a waitress in restaurants and cafes while pursuing her music career. She credits these early jobs for teaching her discipline and how to connect with people, skills she later brought to her performances.

Bathroom Facts - True or False?

1) Toilet seats are cleaner than your smartphone?	True False
2) Toilets flush in different directions in each hemisphere.	True False
3) Toilet water in the U.S. is cleaner than tap water.	True False
4) Some public restrooms play music to deter loitering.	True False
5) Hot water kills all germs on your hands.	True False
6) Ancient Romans used shared sponges as toilet paper.	True False
7) Your toothbrush is at risk from germs if stored near the toilet.	True False
8) All toilets are the same height.	True False
9) The average shower lasts 5 minutes.	True False
10) The term “restroom” was first used in the 20th century.	True False

The text on this page is intentionally upside down to prevent the answers being read accidentally - no spoilers!

Answers: Bathroom Facts - True or False?

1) True - Studies show phones harbor more bacteria because they're handled more frequently without cleaning.

2) False - The Coriolis effect doesn't affect small systems like toilets.

3) False - Toilet water may contain residual germs even if it appears clean.

4) True - High-pitched or classical music is often used to discourage lingering.

5) False - It's the soap and scrubbing that remove germs, not the water temperature.

6) True - Romans used a "tersorium," a communal sponge on a stick, washed in saltwater.

7) True - Toothbrushes can collect airborne bacteria if left uncovered near a flushing toilet.

8) False - Toilets come in various heights to accommodate different needs.

9) False - Surveys show the average shower lasts closer to 8–10 minutes.

10) True - Upscale facilities coined the term to make them sound more elegant.

THE BAGHDAD BATTERY

1

The battery existed before batteries were officially invented. The battery in the form we know it today was thought to have been invented in 1800 by Alessandro Volta, but what if I told you a battery was invented back around 250 B.C.?

2

In 1930, near Baghdad, Iraq, an archaeological relic consisting of a clay jar about 5 inches tall was discovered. Inside, there was a copper cylinder sealed with asphalt and an iron rod inserted into the cylinder, which was also insulated with asphalt. This design, when filled with an acidic liquid such as vinegar, lemon juice, or grape juice, allowed the components to produce an electric current.

3

So what could this battery have been used for? It could have been used to electroplate gold or silver onto objects. Some also suggest it may have served as a source of mild electrical stimulation for therapeutic purposes. It could also have been a symbolic or ritualistic object rather than a functional battery.

4

Some critics argue that there is no evidence that the artifact was used as a battery, and no documented use of electricity or electroplating tools has been found from this period.

5

Regardless of the purpose, the Baghdad battery illustrates the ingenuity of ancient civilizations. It remains a subject of debate, blending archaeology, history, and speculation.

THE MAN IN THE CLOCK

Did you know about the man who lives in a clock? Artist Maarten Baas has a collection called 'Real Time,' which is a series of 12-hour films of performances indicating time, projected inside public clocks.

The first clock project was 'Sweepers,' which was launched in Milan back in 2009. He also released his second one as a special commission at Schiphol Airport in Departures Lounge 2. However, the newest collection is based somewhere special. At one of the major railway stations in London, Paddington, the clock is fully integrated into the building's façade, where a man dressed in a 19th-century-style three-piece suit can be found denoting time minute by minute. This clock's brightness is also determined by the surrounding ambient light conditions.

ANTIKYTHERA MECHANISM

The Antikythera Mechanism is an ancient Greek device often considered the world's **first known analog computer**. It was discovered in 1901 among the wreckage of a ship near the Greek island of Antikythera and dates to around 150–100 BC. At first, it appeared to be a corroded lump of bronze and wood. Its importance was only recognized in 1902 when archaeologist Valerios Stais identified gear-like structures embedded in the artifact.

The device was used to predict astronomical positions and eclipses. It tracked celestial cycles, including the phases of the moon, the positions of the sun and planets, and significant events like the Olympic Games. **But how?**

The mechanism features at least 37 interlocking gears with precise tooth counts to represent celestial cycles. The device had a few functions, including a Zodiac Dial, a solar and lunar calendar, a moon phase indicator, and an eclipse prediction dial. It's believed that the device was able to record and track the five known planet movements as well! This is very impressive for such an ancient society!

So, how did it end up in the sea? Well, the shipwreck that it was found in was thought to be carrying an array of valuables from the Eastern Mediterranean (possibly Rhodes) to Rome at a time when the Romans were interrogating Greek science and technology. How the ship crashed and wrecked is still unknown to historians, but the finding of the device was significant in understanding the scientific effort of the Hellenistic world.

Very Interesting
Animal Facts

Lobster
Lobsters keep their teeth in their stomachs. The teeth are excellent at grinding and are used to break down the shells of their prey.

Wombats
Wombats have cube shaped poo!

Giraffe
Giraffe have the same number of bones in their necks as humans.

Fish
In Honduras, small fish are said to fall from the sky during heavy rains. The event has been observed for over a century and is celebrated as a festival by local people. While the exact cause remains a mystery, theories range from waterspouts lifting fish into the air to fish emerging from underground streams during torrential rains.

Turkeys
When they are scared, or excited, turkeys can blush and the skin on their neck and head changes from its normal pink to red, white. or blue.

Pigs
No one knows how they originally got there but Big Major Cay in the Bahamas is home to about 20 pigs. What's more the pigs love to swim in the sea and are so tame that it is possible for tourists to swim with them and feed them fruit and vegetables whilst they are in the water.

Elephants
Baby elephants comfort themselves by sucking their trunks – adorable!

Remarkable Runestones

It's 1898 in rural Minnesota when Swedish-American farmer Olof Öhman found a large slab of graywacke covered with runic inscriptions. The stone's inscriptions claim a journey by Norse explorers in 1362, detailing a group of Scandinavian travelers who ventured deep into North America. But is all as it seems?

Mysterious Inscriptions

The inscriptions upon the stone consist of runes describing an expedition of thirty Norse explorers, including wedges and Norwegians, who traveled from Vinland (often identified as part of Canada, such as Newfoundland). The stone's runic inscription is written in Scandinavian runes and contains 22 lines of text on the front and a shorter inscription on one edge. Though translations vary among historians and archaeologists, the main message is agreed upon:

"Eight Götalanders and twenty-two Northmen on an exploration journey from Vinland to the west. We had a camp by two shelters, one day's journey north from this stone. We were out fishing one day. When we returned, we found 10 men, red with blood and dead. Ave Maria, save us from evil."

The inscription on the side reads;
"There are 10 men by the sea to look after our ships, 14 days journey from this island year 1362."

Are the claims legitimate?

Believers in the Stone's authenticity argue that the mention of "Ave Maria" indicates the authors of the Stone were of the Christian faith that the Norsemen of the 14th century would have shared. Some scholars also believe that the inability to fully translate the runes could lead to a lack of evidence that the skeptics use against the reliability of the stone. There were also historically recorded explorations of North America pre-Columbian by the Norse.

The skeptics don't agree

But there are also many skeptics who aim to disprove the authenticity of the Stone. For example, linguistic experts analyzed the language, grammar, and structure of the sentences and believe they align more with 19th-century Swedish than with 14th-century Swedish. There is also a significant lack of any other evidence within the entire state of Minnesota of any other Norse expedition, which makes the possibility of the expedition fairly unlikely.
Nonetheless, the Runestone was a striking landmark for Scandinavian immigrants in the Midwest of North America, who strongly believed the Runestone supported their cultural claims on the land. The Runestone can now be found in the Runestone Museum in Alexandria, Minnesota, which celebrates the artifact and its lore, contributing to local tourism.

With all this evidence, what do you believe?

FOREST SECRETS

Redwood National Park is home to the legendary giant redwood trees and amazing wildlife, as well as a few secrets.

Hidden among the beautiful redwoods is a secret radar station built in late 1942 to warn against possible Japanese military strikes.

Though the forest itself could've provided decent enough camouflage, the U.S. Army decided to disguise the radar stations as "farm buildings." They had three buildings altogether, one disguised as a barn, one as a farmhouse, and the third as an outhouse.

Together, they housed radar and anti-aircraft weapons. Though the outhouse is gone now and you can't enter the other buildings due to the security of the structure, you can still view them from the path. Check them out when you next visit the national park.

The Psychic Horse

There was a lovely horse called Lady Wonder who lived in Virginia in the mid-20th century, and she was psychic.

Researchers from Duke University visited the horse to debunk the claims; they wrote words on pieces of paper that Lady Wonder couldn't see and asked her to spell them out, and she did!

However, other investigators thought that the horse's owner was using mentalism tricks then signalling the answers to the horse.

Lady Wonder's owner realized the horse's impeccable talent and created a device for her to communicate by spelling out words, letter by letter.

The horse even helped the police in the case of a missing boy.

Though Lady Wonder gave them a place name that didn't exist, when the deputies rearranged the letters, they visited the location it now spelled out and solved the crime.

When news spread of the horse's skill, people started flocking to her stable from all over the US to ask the horse all sorts of things, from baby genders to sporting bets.
Over 150,000 people visited the horse to seek answers including the outcomes of sporting events and elections.

What an achievement for a horse!

AMAZING!!

Sloths Can Hold Their Breath Longer Than Dolphins

By slowing their heart rate, sloths can hold their breath for up to 40 minutes, while dolphins typically last around 10 minutes.

Rain Contains Dinosaur Pee

Water is part of a continuous cycle on Earth. The water in your glass today has been part of oceans, clouds, and yes, even dinosaur bladders.

The Average Cloud Weighs a Million Pounds

Despite their fluffy appearance, clouds are made of tiny water droplets or ice crystals, making them surprisingly heavy.

Some Turtles Breathe Through Their Butts

Certain species, like the Australian Fitzroy River Turtle, can absorb oxygen through their cloaca, a multi-purpose opening.

Rhinos Communicate Through Poop

Rhinos use their dung to send messages, with specific smells revealing information about their age, sex, and territory.

Rhinos leave their dung in communal piles called middens, which act like social networks for the rhinos.

Never Ask The General Public

(when voting contests go wrong)

In 2012, the soft drinks brand, Mountain Dew launched a marketing campaign called 'Dub The Dew' where it invited the general public to name its famous drink. Popularity of names would be decided by voting. BIG MISTAKE! As well as some offensive political slogans, the Top 10 Leaderboard included the names 'Gushing Granny', 'Tempest', and 'Diabeetus'.

Other voting campaigns elected to

- Get Taylor Swift to play a concert at a school for the deaf. She didn't play there but instead donated a charitable $50,000 to the school.
- Send Justin Beiber to North Korea. As Western music is banned in this country, Justin didn't visit.

In the UK, football club Manchester City ran an online poll to name a stand at it's new ground after one of the club's legends. Colin Bell won the vote but the club quickly realised the stand would acquire the nickname 'The Bell End' so they picked a different name. Colin Bell and his supporters were very annoyed that he had been passed over so the club had to give in and named the side seats after the player in an attempt to keep everyone happy.

In 1967, the students at the University of Colorado were canvassed about a name for their new dining hall. Voting ensued and the name picked was Alferd Packer who was a known cannibal from 1874.

Nearly a quarter of a million people voted to name a node of the Space Station and the winning name was 'Colbert' after a comedian named Stephen Colbert urged fans to vote to use his name. Nasa decided to ignore this and call the node Tranquility instead but in order to prevent upset, they named a treadmill on the Space Station after Colbert. It's called the **C**ombined **O**perational **L**oad **B**earing **E**xternal **R**esistance **T**readmill.

NAMES PEOPLE USE for the Bathroom

V.I.P BATHROOMS

KOHLER NUMI 2.0 SMART TOILET

This incredible toilet boasts amazing features, making it one of the top options available. It includes voice-activated controls, a heated seat, ambient lighting, and a built-in Bluetooth speaker. Additionally, it comes with advanced self-cleaning technologies using UV lights and electrolyzed water. And what's even better? It provides a touchless experience with motion sensors.

A CRYSTAL CLEAR POTTY

In Shiyanhu Ecological Park in Changsha, Hunan Province, China, there is a remarkable public restroom. The toilet is constructed entirely of glass—glass walls, floors, and ceiling—making the user almost exposed to the elements. However, this design offers an incredible view while you do your business. To alleviate privacy concerns, the dividing walls and doors between individual stalls are made of frosted one-way glass. The facility is solar-powered, which aligns with the park's ecological theme.

THE DIAMOND TOILET

Palazzo d'Accursio in Bologna, Italy, is home to the Diamond Toilet. This toilet, known as 'America,' was created by Italian artist Maurizio Cattelan in 2016. It is adorned with thousands of diamonds and valued at millions of dollars. Unlike the toilet made of pure gold, this one is regarded as a piece of conceptual art rather than a functional restroom fixture. Would you use a diamond-encrusted toilet?

THE TOILET IN THE SKY

The Sky Garden Toilet, located in the Park Hyatt Tokyo, is remarkably unique. Situated on the top floors of the hotel, users can enjoy panoramic views of Mount Fuji and Tokyo's skyline. The bathroom boasts gold-plated taps, high-end marble, and luxurious amenities. The combination of extravagant fixtures and stunning views makes this bathroom one for the history books.

DID YOU KNOW?

A bear served the army during World War II

Have you heard of the Bear who served during World War II? Wojtech the Bear was a Syrian brown bear who was found as an orphaned cub by Polish soldiers in Iran. The soldiers decided to take him in and raise him among them, so he quickly became part of their unit. Wojtek was formally enlisted as a private in the Polish II Corps; his role included carrying supplies and ammunition. After the war ended, he was relocated to Edinburgh Zoo, where he happily lived out the rest of his life.

DID YOU KNOW?

There was a real life Baloo

There was a real-life Baloo bear that inspired the character of the same name in “The Jungle Book.” Baloo was a bear who performed in circuses and was the star of a series of popular films. He amassed his fame from his gentle nature, and many say his kind demeanor served as inspiration for the bear in Rudyard Kipling’s book. The bear was said to belong to a circus in the United States and lived from 1916 to 1939.

Fun Flying Facts

Toilet Troubles

Did you know that there's a secret latch to open the toilets on planes from the outside? Flight Attendants and other airline crew are taught about this little secret in the case of an emergency. Depending on the type of plane, the latch can be hidden under the toilet sign itself or under the 'No Smoking' sign.

Double Toilet Trouble

Did you know that on some aircraft, they can open the wall between toilets? On a Boeing 787, the middle set of toilets in the mid cabin are separated by a thin panel. This panel can be folded away to allow space for two people or a wheelchair more easily. There is a latch in the top corner that needs to be opened by the crew onboard. This is usually saved for special circumstances only and is not routinely used.

Oxygen Doesn't Last Forever

Did you know that the Oxygen masks that drop down in the case of a decompression don't last forever? Depending on the aircraft the oxygen will last between 12-22 minutes. Don't panic! The oxygen system only provides the oxygen until the plane can descend to a breathable altitude, not till the plane lands. You can breathe normally once the plane descends to a lower altitude, where you'll most likely stay until you can land safely.

The Chicken Gun of Flight Safety

Did you know that they test the durability of the plane's engine against bird strikes by using a chicken gun? Now, unfortunately, this is exactly what it sounds like: a cannon that shoots dead chickens or other debris with precision toward the aircraft. Don't worry, though. The chickens are already dead and are sometimes even frozen. Though it seems barbaric, this is key safety testing to keep the airplanes as safe as they can be.

"Where do you live?"

(embarrassing answers)

USA

Boring, Oregon

Truth or Consequences, New Mexico

Lick Skillet, Alabama

Pee Pee, Ohio

Two Egg, Florida

Burnt Corn, Alabama

Ticklebelly Hill, Nebraska

UK

Piddlehinton, Dorset

Wetwang, East Yorkshire

Twatt, Orkney and Shetland Islands

Ugley, Essex

Thong, Kent

Scratchy Bottom, Dorset

Australia

Useless Loop, Western Australia

Nowhere Else, Tasmania

Eggs and Bacon Bay, Tasmania

Poo Wong, Victoria

Canada

Saint-Louis-du-Ha! Ha!, Quebec

Spuzzum, British Columbia

Balls Creek, Nova Scotia

Other Countries

Batman, Turkey

Disappointment Island, New Zealand

Middlefart, Denmark

Moron, Mongolia

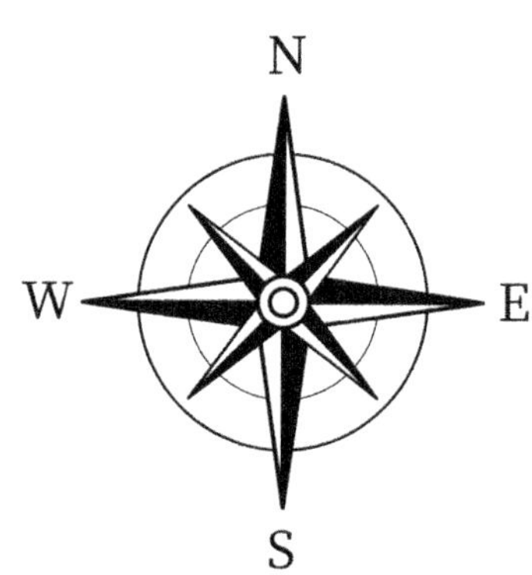

Dismaland

Did you hear about the dystopian "anti-amusement park" created by Banksy? Dismaland was a temporary satirical take on theme parks and consumer culture created by the political British artist Banksy.

Dismaland was located in Weston-super-Mare in England, in what used to be an outdoor swimming pool. The park was open to the public for a month, attracting thousands of visitors from across the UK.

The installation was a parody of Disneyland with a dark, surreal twist on classic theme park attractions. It featured unsettling art, grotesque sculptures, and social commentary on issues like consumerism, environmental destruction, and political corruption. The experience was intentionally designed to provoke thought rather than provide enjoyment; however, the attraction was very entertaining for those who visited.

Banksy was not the only artist; in fact, he invited over fifty other artists from around the world to partake. Some of the most famous pieces included a dystopian version of Cinderella, a Helter Skelter ride with an unsettling atmosphere, and a police car being submerged in water.

Dismaland received varied reactions, with some loving its dark humor and others disturbed by this. However, it was widely praised for its originality and subversive approach to art.

NUTTY NAMES

- Couch Potato
- Butterfingers
- Cheeseball
- Egghead
- Sweetie Pie
- Big Cheese
- Tough Cookie
- Bad Apple
- Cherry Picker
- Plum Job
- Fruitcake
- Honey Bunny
- Cookie Cutter
- Beefcake
- Chowhound
- Salt of the Earth
- Tater Tot
- Cup of Joe
- Milkshake
- Espresso Yourself
- Smoothie
- Gravy Train
- Salty
- Top Banana
- Peach Fuzz
- Brownie Points
- Candy Coated
- Sloppy Joe
- Spud
- Onion Layered

Foodie Facts

Peaches were the first food eaten on the moon!

After capturing historic photos on the Moon, Armstrong and Aldrin shared a meal. Their first meal included peaches as well as cubed bacon, sugar cookies, pineapple-grapefruit juice, and coffee.

There's a cheese that contains live maggots!

Casu marzu, or "maggot cheese," is a Sardinian delicacy made from sheep's milk and fermented with live cheese fly larvae. The resulting maggots develop the cheese, creating a creamy texture and a strong, tangy flavor. Disgustingly, the cheese is often eaten with the maggots still wriggling although this is technically illegal in the European Union due to health concerns.

There's a coffee made by a pooping cat!

Kopi Luwak, or "poop coffee," is made from coffee beans that have been eaten and pooped out by the Asian palm civet cat. The cat's digestive process ferments the beans which is thought to improve the taste of the coffee. After being defecated, the beans are collected, thankfully cleaned, and roasted to create this famously unusual brew.

A miracle berry can make sour food taste sweet!

The miracle berry is a small red fruit native to West Africa that has an extraordinary effect on the way we taste food. After eating the berry, its active compound, miraculin, binds to taste buds and temporarily alters the way sour flavors are perceived, making foods like lemons and vinegar taste sweet. This natural "flavor trip" can last up to an hour.

A publicity stunt was used to promote potatoes!

In the 18th century a French pharmacist thought potatoes were good for you and wanted to promote them. He persuaded the King to lend him some land which he duely planted with potatoes. He surrounded the land with armed guards to make people think that the crop was valuable. The guards were then given orders to allow thieves to steal the potatoes and also to accept any bribes that were offered. The thefts helped to make potatoes popular and save the French people from famine.

ANIMAL GROUPS

A Murder of Crows

A Flamboyance of Flamingos

A Crash of Rhinos

A Mob of Emus

An Ambush of Tigers

A Tower of Giraffes

A Cackle of Hyenas

A Memory of Elephants

Toynbee Tiles

The Toynbee Tiles are mysterious street plaques embedded in asphalt across dozens of cities in North and South America, primarily the United States. First appearing in the 1980s, they are known for their cryptic messages and unknown origin.

The Tiles that are no bigger than a license plate have an array of messages but the most popular and repeated message is:
"TOYNBEE IDEA IN MOViE 2001 RESURRECT DEAD ON PLANET JUPITER"

But what could it mean?

There are a few theories:

1. **The Toynbee Idea** - Many people believe this refers to British historian Arnold J. Toynbee, whose primary legacy lies in his theories about the cyclical rise and fall of civilizations.
2. **The 2001 Space Odyssey Idea** - Regarding 'MOVIE 2001' many believe this is about the movie based on Arthur C. Clarke's work which explores themes of human evolution and extraterrestrial life.
3. **The Resurrect Dead on Planet Jupiter Idea** - This idea suggests the tiles could be talking about the idea of human resurrection on the planet Jupiter after Earth fails.

But where did they come from?

The tiles are found embedded in streets, likely placed using tar and paper and fixed in place by the pressure of vehicles passing over them.

Despite the tiles' public display, their creator has never been revealed, though an odd clue exists. Many believe the tiles are the work of a single artist, likely from the Philadelphia area, as that's where the majority of tiles come from.

Amazing Things To Tell Your Friends

A sloth's digestive process can take weeks. Their metabolism is so slow that it can take up to a month to digest a single meal.

Sea otters hold hands while sleeping to keep from drifting apart while floating on the water's surface.

Tardigrades, a micro animal, can survive in space. These tiny creatures can endure extreme conditions, including the vacuum of space and intense radiation.

Starfish can regrow their arms. If they lose an arm, they can regenerate it, and in some cases, an entire new starfish can grow from a severed arm.

Butterflies can taste with their feet, allowing them to detect food sources by landing on them.

Octopuses have three hearts. Two pump blood to the gills, and one pumps it to the rest of the body.

ANIMAL SPIES

1 Hvaldimir the Whale Spy

Hvaldimir, named by the Norwegian fisherman who noticed him, is a pun between hval (whale in Norwegian) and Vladimir (for Russian president Vladimir Putin). He was a whale that was recognized in 2019 as wearing a tight-fitting camera harness labeled 'Equipment St Petersburg.' The whale was caught brushing up against the sides of the fishermen's boats, a motion that they speculated was an effort to remove the spy equipment. A Russian spokesperson has claimed that they don't use whales as spies, but their use of them in combat could suggest otherwise. Either way, Hvaldimir has spent the last few years just off the coast of Norway, possibly intending to defect to the enemy.

2 Going Nuts

What small animal that usually goes unnoticed would make an excellent spy? Well, according to the Iranian Army, squirrels fit the bill! In 2007, they arrested 14 squirrels whom they believed were working for the Americans by wearing small recording devices. Though the CIA denied this spy network as 'complete idiocy'.

3 The Smartest Mammals

The Russians have been accused of some pretty crazy spying techniques, and this is one of them!
In 2018, it emerged that the Russian Navy supposedly sent trained dolphins to support their war in Syria. Researchers believe that the dolphins would likely be used to counter the enemy divers who would interfere with Russian ships.

4 Man's Best Spy

It was during WWII that British army officers had some crazy suspicions. They witnessed two cats and a dog constantly passing through the trenches at night. Though they tried to grab hold of them, their records do not say whether the animals were detained or not. To this day, we do not know if the animals were really spies.

5 The Flying Chinese Spy

After eight long months spent in jail, a pigeon suspected of being a Chinese Spy was finally released in 2024. The poor pigeon had a lengthy service at Mumbai's Hospital for Animals. It was detained after being caught near Mumbai port with two rings tied to its legs and writing that seemed to be Chinese. The innocent creature was later discovered to be a Taiwanese open-water racing bird that had escaped and flown to India. This poor fellow was not India's first wrongly accused pigeon; one was arrested after being found with a note that threatened Indian Prime Minister Narendra Modi. It's strange that it happened twice.

RANDOM FACTS

Cleopatra lived closer in time to the iPhone than the pyramids.

The Great Pyramid of Giza was built around 2560 BCE, while Cleopatra lived closer to 0 CE.

You can walk from Russia to Alaska in Winter.

The Bering Strait freezes over in some years, creating a natural ice bridge between the two countries.

There's a secret train station under the Waldorf Astoria in NYC.

It was built for President Franklin D. Roosevelt to travel discreetly.

The voices of Mickey Mouse and Minnie Mouse were married in real life.

Wayne Allwine (Mickey) and Russi Taylor (Minnie) were married for 18 years until Wayne's passing in 2009.

THE WOW SIGNAL

In August 1977, astronomer Jerry R. Ehman detected something special when using the Big Ear radio telescope at Ohio State University.

No one truly knows how long the signal lasted, as the telescope that measured it could only assess to a maximum of 72 seconds. However, the signal lasted at least that length of time. The signal originated in the direction of the Sagittarius constellation near the star cluster of Chi Sagittarii. The intensity of the signal was significantly higher than the background noise, indicating a very strong and narrowband transmission.

So, where did the name "The Wow Signal" come from? Well, when observing and listening to the transmission, Jerry R. Ehman famously wrote 'Wow!' in the margins of the printout, recording the signal and unknowingly giving it its lasting name.

What could explain this phenomenon? The narrowband signal and its frequency of 1420MHz, which is the natural radio frequency of hydrogen, hint at the possibility of extraterrestrial intelligence. Hydrogen, a universal element, is considered an ideal marker for interstellar communication, leading to speculation that the signal could have an artificial origin.

Some believe a natural phenomenon like pulsars, comets, or interstellar gas clouds could have caused the transmitted sound. Some strong skeptics believe that the sound was interference from satellites or Earth-based equipment, though it's unlikely.

Since the transmission was first recorded in 1977, subsequent searches in the same area failed to detect the signal again. In 2017 researcher Antonio Paris proposed that the signal was caused by a passing comet, but this theory is widely debated.

STUPENDOUS SURVIVAL STORIES

EVEREST

In May 2006, Lincoln Hall collapsed whilst descending Everest. His Sherpas tried to revive him but eventually gave up. Thinking he was dead, the Sherpas took Hall's gear including his oxygen. Next morning, another expedition found Hall sitting up, alive, in the snow. He says he survived thanks to a 'don't give up' mindset.

AIR CRASH

In 1972, flight attendant Vesna Vulović survived a 33,000-foot fall when a bomb exploded on her plane over Czechoslovakia. Though she suffered multiple fractures and injuries, she miraculously recovered and holds the Guinness World Record for the highest fall without a parachute.

LOST AT SEA

In 1981, Steven Callahan's sailboat sank during a solo voyage across the Atlantic. He survived for 76 days in a small life raft, drinking rainwater and catching fish with makeshift tools. His ordeal ended when he was rescued by fishermen near the Caribbean.

FROZEN SOLID

In 1999, Swedish radiologist Anna Bågenholm fell into an icy stream while skiing. She was trapped for 80 minutes in freezing water, and her body temperature dropped to 56.7°F (13.7°C). Despite being clinically dead, doctors revived her, and she made a full recovery.

MARATHON

In 1994, Italian runner Mauro Prosperi got lost in a sandstorm during the Marathon des Sables in the Sahara Desert. He survived for nine days by drinking his own urine, eating bats, and seeking shelter in an abandoned mosque before being rescued.

Museum Marvels

The David Tennant Banknote

There are several amazing displays within the British Museum, but one in particular is special. In celebration of the British actor David Tennant, the Royal Mint created a fictional £10 note that has become popular among fans due to its unique design. Key features include a central portrait of David Tennant and subtle references to his Doctor Who tenure, such as the TARDIS and Gallifreyan symbols. This banknote is a limited edition, produced in small quantities, making it a collector's item. It is purely commemorative and cannot be used as legal tender.

Jar of Giant Moles

Did you know that the Grant Museum of Zoology in Bloomsbury, London, has a fascinating display of a 'Jar of Giant Moles'? The jar contains the preserved bodies of the European mole but on a larger-than-usual scale. The specimens are submerged in preserving fluid, making them look eerie and captivating. The moles aren't unnaturally large; they're just grouped in such a way that they appear larger and more unusual than expected. However, the oddity and quirkiness of the display have garnered attention from all across the globe. It is definitely worth checking out when you next visit London!

William 'Bumper' Harris's Walking Stick

Have you ever heard of the story of William 'Bumper' Harris? William Harris, nicknamed "Bumper", was a one-legged man known for his work in promoting London Underground escalators when they were first introduced. Harris was hired to ride up and down the first-ever Underground escalator to ease public fears. He did an amazing job proving that even someone with mobility challenges could easily use the escalators. The walking stick used by Harris became a symbol of his efforts and resilience. It is currently on display at the London Transport Museum in Covent Garden.

Wonderful Words

Lackadaisical – Lacking enthusiasm and determination; carelessly lazy.

Scuttlebutt – Gossip or rumor.

Floccinaucinihilipilification – Estimating something as worthless.

Pluviophile – A person who loves the sound and feel of rain.

Mellifluous – Sweet or musical; pleasant to hear.

Obfuscate – To render obscure, unclear, or unintelligible.

Discombobulate – To confuse or disconcert; upset; frustrate.

Apoplectic – Overcome with anger; extremely indignant.

Dysania – The state of finding it hard to get out of bed in the morning.

Widdershins – In a direction contrary to the sun's course; counterclockwise.

Xenophobia – Dislike of or prejudice against people from other countries.

Borborygmus – The rumbling sound produced by gas in the intestines.

Hobbledehoy – A clumsy or awkward young person.

Collywobbles – Stomach pain or queasiness.

Bloviate – To talk at length, especially in a pompous way.

Gobbledygook – Language that is meaningless; jargon.

CURIOUS CIPHERS

Thomas J. Beale, the author of this mystery, entrusted a box containing three encoded messages to Robert Morriss, an innkeeper. Beale left instructions and a promise that a key would eventually be delivered to Morriss to decipher the codes, however, the key never arrived. Thus the mystery of the Beale cipher was born.

The box contains three ciphertexts:

- Cipher 1 - Describes the exact location of the treasure.
- Cipher 2 - Lists the contents of the treasure.
- Cipher 3 - Provides the names of the heirs to the treasure.

While the first and third ciphers remain a mystery, one of Morriss' anonymous friends is said to have solved the second cipher. This friend used the Declaration of Independence as the key and, in doing so, uncovered a long list resembling a treasure inventory. It is rumored that the treasure is worth over $60 million in today's value. Despite numerous attempts by cryptographers, treasure hunters, and enthusiasts, the first and third ciphers remain unsolved.

Some believe the story that the ciphers are genuine and that the treasure is simply awaiting discovery. Others argue the entire tale is a 19th-century fabrication by Morriss or his friends to help them sell pamphlets and claim their moment of fame. Some theorize the ciphers are intentionally unsolvable suggesting that there was never a key in the first place.

71, 194, 38, 1701, 89, 76,11, 83, 1629, 48,
94, 63, 132, 16, 111, 95, 84, 341, 975, 14,
40, 64, 27, 81,139, 213, 63, 90, 1120, 8,
15, 3, 126, 2018, 40, 74, 758, 485, 604,
230, 436, 664, 582, 150, 251, 284, 308,
231, 124, 211, 486, 225, 401, 370, 11, 101,
305, 139, 189, 17, 33, 88, 208, 193, 145, 1,
94, 73, 416, 918, 263, 28, 500, 538, 356,
117, 136, 219, 27, 176, 130, 10, 460, 25,
485, 18, 436, 65, 84, 200, 283, 118, 320,
138, 36, 416, 280, 15, 71, 224, 961, 44,
16, 401, 39, 88, 61, 304, 12, 21, 24, 283

THE CURSED GRAVE

William Shakespeare, the renowned playwright, is buried in Holy Trinity Church in Stratford-upon-Avon, his hometown. Despite his fame and incredible legacy, Shakespeare is buried alongside his family, with a fairly modest epitaph marking his burial place.

What makes this burial so unique is the inscription on his epitaph, which hints at supernatural consequences for those who disturb his final resting place.

The inscription is as follows:
'Good friend for Jesus' sake forbear,
To dig the dust enclosed here.
Blessed be the man that spares these stones,
And cursed be he that moves my bones.'

The fear of this curse has prevented any exhumation or detailed examination of Shakespeare's remains. However, in 2016, a radar survey suggested that the skull might be missing; nevertheless, the grave itself has remained untouched due to the curse.

But why did he leave this world with such a threatening last message? The curse could reflect Shakespeare's possible concern about posthumous grave disturbance, a common practice at the time.

Whatever the reason, the inscription adds an air of mystery to his legacy and has become a point of fascination for both visitors and scholars.

SCIENCE STORIES

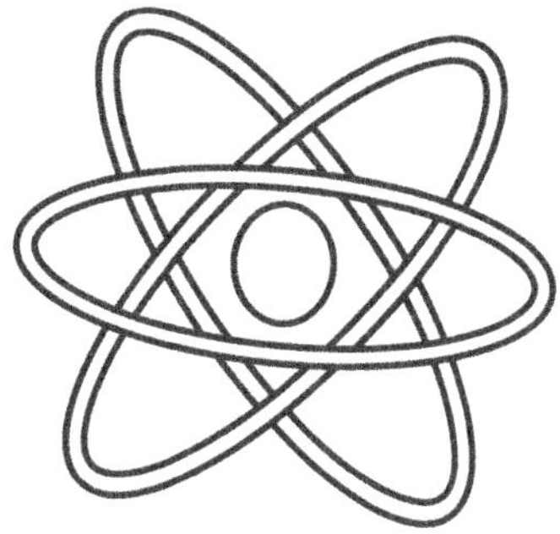

- Scottish scientists are working on a way to use LED bulbs as Internet transmitters that would be faster and more secure than the current wifi. The network of light transmitters would be dubbed 'Li-Fi'.

- One of the reasons NASA picked Florida as a launch site because of its proximity to the equator. The Earth rotates at a higher speed at the equator than the poles so this extra velocity means that rockets use less energy to overcome gravity and get into orbit.

- Doctors don't fully understand why anesthetics work. There are lots of hypotheses but scientists cannot agree on the way anesthetic reduces the loss of sensation and consciousness. There are probably a variety of reasons which work together rather than one simple process.

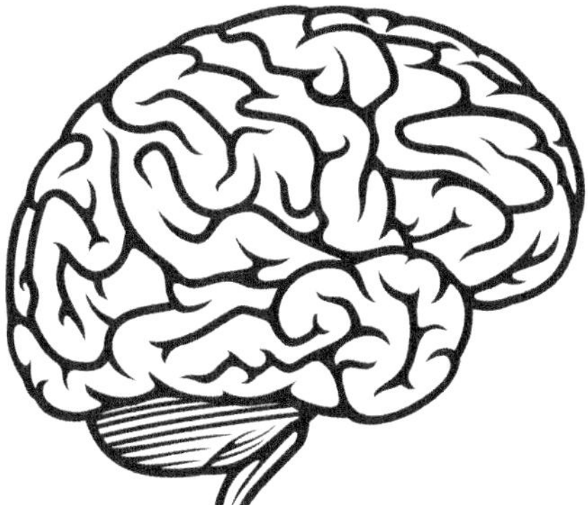

- The rays of sunlight that you see today were first generated by the sun 100,000 years ago. It takes the photons that long to reach the surface of the sun. Once on the surface, it only takes an additional 8 minutes and 26 seconds to get to Earth.

FUNNY SIGNS

THE INVENTOR OF AUTOCORRECT DIED. THE FUNNEL WILL BE HELD TOMATO.

THOSE WHO THROW OBJECTS AT THE CROCODILES WILL BE ASKED TO RETREIVE THEM

DRIVE LIKE THE PERSON YOUR DOG THINKS YOU ARE

IN CASE OF FIRE

EXIT BUILDING BEFORE POSTING ON SOCIAL MEDIA

NO PARKING.

THE LAST PERSON WHO PARKED HERE IS STILL REPORTED MISSING.

DO NOT CLIMB THE FENCE. THE ANIMALS MIGHT EAT YOU AND THAT WOULD MAKE THEM SICK.

WARNING: UNATTENDED CHILDREN WILL BE GIVEN AN ESPRESSO WITH LOTS OF SUGAR

BOMB ON A BUS

(and other incredible tales)

The CIA has made many mistakes, some that have been very public, and some that are probably still secret. One was in 2016, when the CIA was conducting a training exercise for bomb-sniffing dogs on a school bus. The dogs were supposed to locate explosive material hidden on the bus, but at some point, a portion of the explosive material became dislodged from the container it was held in. This explosive material fell into the engine compartment of the bus and was not recovered following the end of the training. The bus in question was also still in use by a local high school and was driving around with kids on board while the material went unnoticed. Thankfully, no one was hurt, and the material was retrieved during the following training session

New Mexico is a special state for many reasons. New Mexico has a state bird, the greater roadrunner, and a state flower, the yucca, as nearly every U.S. state shares these two attributes. But New Mexico does have something that no other state has: a state question. The question is in regard to what kind of chile pepper someone wants, so their official state question is: "Red or green?" which has been official since 1996. The state also wants to further its distinction by adopting a state aroma. The proposed smell would be "green chiles roasting in the fall."

INCREDIBLE!

In the 1500s, a court jester took a joke too far when he playfully slapped the King on his bottom. He followed this up with a joke about mistaking the King for the Queen which made the King even more furious. The jester was sentenced to death. However, the King told the jester he could decide his method of execution. The Jester chose to die 'of old age' and the King was so impressed by his answer that he decided to banish the jester from Court to the countryside where he could live out his life in peace.

PERILOUS PROFESSIONS

If a Prince, who was still a child, needed punishment for bad behavior, then another boy had the job of receiving corporal punishment. His job title was 'whipping boy'. He would always need to stay close to the Prince, so they often grew up as friends.

Medical students required dead bodies that they could study for anatomical purposes. Thus, the profession of 'resurrectionists' or 'body snatchers' came about. Under the cover of darkness, the job was to steal dead bodies from graves and sell them on.

A 'pure finder' had the disgusting job of searching the streets for dog poop which they collected and sold on to tanners. The dog poop was used to soften leather so that it could be worked into footwear.

Wool fullers were required to make the woolly fabric softer to the touch. To do this, they had to stomp on the fabric with their bare feet using a soaking liquid of urine, as the ammonium salts in the stale urine helped to soften the cloth and also bleached it white.

In the 19th century, leech collectors waded through marshes and ponds, letting blood-sucking leeches attach to their legs so they could gather them for medical use. In addition to painful bites, they risked blood loss, infections, and diseases.

FELICITY ACE

CARGO SHIP

$400M

AT THE BOTTOM OF THE ATLANTIC OCEAN

The Felicity Ace was a Panama-flagged cargo ship specifically built to carry thousands of vehicles. Tragically, catastrophe struck during a trip from Germany to the United States.

A fire broke out on board as the ship was near the Azores, a group of islands off the coast of Portugal. Thankfully, all 22 crew members were successfully evacuated. However, the fire continued to burn for days to come, fueled by the lithium-ion batteries in some of the electric cars.

At the time, the ship was carrying approximately 4,000 vehicles, most of which were luxury brands like Porsche, Audi, Bentley, and Lamborghini.

Due to the nature of the batteries within these high-value electric cars, the fire was nearly impossible to extinguish.

Three weeks later, while being towed, the ship sank to about 3,000 meters deep in the Atlantic Ocean, carrying with it the precious cargo of rare and custom vehicles.

2005

The sinking not only had a great effect on the personal economy of the car owners and the transportation company, but also had a greater environmental effect on the ocean. There were concerns about pollution from oil, debris, and hazardous materials, including the lithium-ion batteries within some of the electric cars.

The event highlighted the risks of transporting electric vehicles and the challenges of handling battery-related fires in maritime environments.

TREASURES in the trash

The collection features

Nelson Molina, a retired New York City sanitation worker, opened The Treasures in the Trash Museum in 2015, showcasing valuable, unusual, and historical items salvaged from the garbage over the three decades he worked there.

The museum is housed within an unused section of the New York City Department of Sanitation garage in East Harlem. Molina worked for the NYC Department of Sanitation for 34 years. At first, he started his collection as a personal project, driven by uncovering hidden value in the discarded items.

His colleagues began adding weird pieces to the collection and the idea caught on.

Molina organizes the pieces by size, general theme, and color.

Access for the public is by request only but sanitation workers are allowed in at any time.

Brilliant Bananas

- Bananas can float in water.
- Over 100 billion bananas are eaten every year as they are the World's most popular fruit.
- There are over 1,000 varieties of banana.
- Rubbing the inside of a banana peel on your skin can relieve the itching from an insect bite.
- You can use the inside of a banana peel as a polish for leather shoes. The natural oils and potassium condition the leather.
- August 25th is National Banana Split Day.
- The word 'banana' is thought to come from the Arabic word 'banan,' meaning finger.
- The banana split was invented in 1904 by a pharmacist in Pennsylvania.
- Banana peel is edible and are used in cooking in some cultures.
- Bananas are rich in potassium, which can help prevent muscle cramps.
- Bananas emit ethylene gas, which speeds up the ripening process for themselves and other fruits nearby.
- Despite the stereotype, bananas are not a staple food for most wild monkeys.
- Bananas contain tryptophan, which can help the body produce serotonin, a mood-enhancing hormone.
- Bananas come in a range of colors, including red, pink, purple, and green.
- A banana plant produces only one bunch of bananas in its lifetime before the main stalk dies and a new one grows.

Never Ask The General Public

(when voting contests go wrong)

Traditonally, snowplows and salting trucks are named for each season with members of the public suggesting names. These are some of the winners:

- Beyonsleigh
- Fast and Flurrious
- Yer a Blizzard, Harry
- Clearopathtra
- Han Snowlo
- Sleetwood Mac
- Plowsaurus Rex
- Blizzard of Oz
- Edward Blizzardhands
- Plowy McPlowFace
- Snowbi Wan Kenobi
- F. Salt Fitzgerald
- Veruca Salt
- Salt Disney
- Lord Coldemort
- Licence to Chill
- Darth Blader
- Gritter Thunberg
- Gritty Gritty Bang Bang
- Sir David Attenbrrrr
- Buzz Saltyear
- No More Mr Ice Guy
- Ctrl Salt Delete
- Snowbegone
- Kaenu Freeze
- Taylor Drift
- Skate Bush
- Melter Skelter
- The Gritternator
- Hansel and Grit-all
- Salta Claus
- I Want To Break Freeze
- Spready Mercury
- Chicken Plow Main
- Sweet Child O'Brine
- Don't Flurry Be Happy
- I Snow You Can Do It
- Ka-Plow!
- The Mayplower
- Snow Monstah
- Marco Plowo
- Snowprah Winfrey
- Blizzo
- Cirque du Snowleil
- Nevada Thaw Enforcement
- Melton John
- Scoop Dog
- Best in Snow
- The Truck Formerly Known As Plow

Weird Museums

The Paris Sewer Museum educates people about the industrial sewer complex that lies beneath their feet and tells the story of the sewermen who clean and maintain the sewers.
The museum is set in an actual, functioning sewer and can be a little smelly!

Conspiracy theorists will love the International UFO museum in Roswell, New Mexico.
The museum pitches itself as the leading source of information about worldwide UFO events.
It has replica alien corpses and reports on crop circles and supposed UFO crashes and alien abductions.

The Museum of Salt and Pepper Shakers in Gatlinburg, Tennessee, showcases over 20,000 pairs of shakers from around the globe.

How much would you like to know about rabbits?
You can check out over 35,000 displays at The Bunny Museum in California.
Visitors can admire everything bunny related from ceramic rabbits, stuffed rabbits and even a few live rabbits.

The Spy Museum in Washington D.C. holds a fascinating array of exhibits including the tools need to plant a bug or communicate in a covert manner.
The museum also contains stories about famous spies, runs code cracking challenges, and has had special, exhibitions including 007 Bond cars.

The Banana Museum in Mecca, California, now closed, began with banana stickers and grew as fans sent in artifacts to be put on display for visitors to admire.
Contributors became members of the Banana Club, which eventually boasted 35,000 members across 17 countries.

Fun Findings

The first kids' toy ever to be advertised on TV was Mr Potato Head.

Analogue watches for sale have thier hands set to 10:10 to mimic a smiley face.

Charlie Chaplin once entered a look-a-like contest as himself but was sadly only placed 3rd.

The first baby stroller was created to transport a goat rather than a human baby.

The Romans used powdered mouse brains as a primative toothpaste.

Bubble wrap was originally invented as insulating wallpaper.

THE SECRET OF THE *Great Seal*

It was 1945 when Soviet schoolchildren presented a carved wooden replica of the United States Great Seal to the U.S. Ambassador to the Soviet Union as a 'gesture of goodwill.' The carving was hung in the U.S. Embassy in Moscow, and the U.S. Embassy didn't realize contained a hidden listening device.

The passive listening device, known as The Thing, was designed by Leon Theremin, a Soviet inventor and the creator of the Theremin instrument. What made The Thing so impressive was that it was nearly undetectable. It did not have a power source, so it was unlikely to be picked up using standard bug-sweeping techniques. Instead, it was activated remotely using a directed radio signal. Once activated, the device picked up conversations within the room and transmitted them to Soviet intelligence.

It remained hidden for seven years before being discovered in 1952 during a lucky security sweep. The Thing is now in the Spy Museum in Washington, a symbol of Cold War ingenuity and a key feature in the museum's collection, showcasing the history of intelligence and espionage.

Spectacular Species

Bombardier Beetle

This beetle sprays a boiling, noxious chemical mixture from its abdomen as a defense mechanism. The liquid reaches temperatures of 100°C (212°F) and is expelled with an audible popping sound to ward off predators.

Coconut Crab

The coconut crab, can weigh up to 9 pounds and climb trees. It's powerful enough to crack open coconuts with its claws and has been known to scavenge anything it finds, including discarded pots and pans.

Echidna

This spiny mammal lays eggs like a reptile but nurses its young with milk. Its tongue can flick out 100 times per minute to scoop up ants and termites, making it one of nature's most efficient bug-eaters.

Cassowary

The cassowary is the world's most dangerous bird, capable of killing humans with a single kick. Its dagger-like claw can grow up to 5 inches long, and it runs at speeds up to 31 miles per hour through dense forests.

Vampire Bats

These bats are the only mammals that feed exclusively on blood. They've evolved a heat-sensing nose to locate blood vessels on their prey and can drink undetected thanks to an anticoagulant in their saliva.

EXTREME EXCREMENT

1 Bird and bat droppings, known as guano, were once one of the world's most valuable fertilizers due to their high nitrogen and phosphorus content. In the 19th century, nations competed over guano-rich islands, leading to the Guano Islands Act of 1856, which allowed the U.S. to claim uninhabited islands for their deposits.

2 Wombats, native to Australia, produce cube-shaped poop! This bizarre adaptation helps prevent their droppings from rolling away, allowing them to use their feces to mark their territory effectively. The unique shape is due to the varying elasticity of their intestinal walls.

3 Dung beetles are expert recyclers of animal excrement, and some species use the Milky Way for navigation. At night, they roll dung balls in straight lines using the light of the stars as a guide, an incredible feat of celestial orientation.

4 Elephants produce massive amounts of dung—up to 300 pounds per day—and their diet is rich in fibrous plant material. This makes their excrement an excellent source for making eco-friendly paper, a sustainable alternative used for souvenirs and stationery in countries like Thailand and Sri Lanka.

5 Koalas produce up to 100 droppings a day, which may seem mundane until you learn that their poop helps juvenile koalas, or joeys, develop a tolerance for eucalyptus leaves. Joeys eat a special type of their mother's poop called "pap," which contains beneficial bacteria.

6 Sloths climb down to the ground only once a week to poop in the same spot each time. This behavior fertilizes the ground below their trees, creating a "poop garden" that nourishes plants and even supports insects that live in their fur, forming a unique ecosystem.

7 Termites use their poop to construct their intricate and massive mounds. Their droppings act as a natural cement, binding soil and creating structures with built-in ventilation systems to regulate temperature.

NIFTY NAMES

ZEEDONK
An animal created by breeding a zebra and a donkey.

INTERROBANG
The term for a question mark immediately followed by an exclamation mark ?!

CREEPER
The name of the first ever computer worm, created in 1971. A computer worm is a type of malware that can spread though a computer network without human intervention

TOUCH
Touch was the original name of the Spice Girls, who were given the individual names Ginger, Sporty, Posh, Scary, and Baby by Top of Pops.

SKIPPER, STACIE, & CHELSEA
The names of Barbie's three younger sisters.

CADABRA
The original name of Amazon. Cadabra was the name of an online bookstore and was incorporated in 1995. It went on to become Amazon.

SID
The real name of the Cookie Monster in the Muppets.

THE MAMMOTH MEATBALL

Scientists from Eat Just Inc., a food technology company, created something amazing in 2021.

The Woolly Mammoth is an extinct species that roamed the Earth during the Ice Age. Using the mammoth's genetic material, the scientists aimed to understand how to grow the meat of an extinct animal through biotechnology. Using mammoth DNA extracted from ancient specimens, the scientists synthesized the DNA and employed it to create muscle cells, essentially cultivating the meat in the lab.

The initiative was part of an effort to explore cultured meat and how biotechnology can recreate the meat of extinct species. It also served as a demonstration of how this technology might be used to address environmental and ethical concerns related to traditional meat production. There are currently questions regarding sustainability and conservation as this form of lab-grown meat could be an alternative to traditionally grown livestock, potentially reducing environmental impact.

The company showcased the final mammoth meatball. Though it was not intended for human consumption at the time, it symbolized a huge step in food technology and genetic research.

Outer Space

There are more stars in the Universe than there are grains of sand on Earth.
Astronomers estimate that there are about 1 septillion (1,000,000,000,000,000,000,000,000) stars in the universe, vastly outnumbering all the grains of sand on Earth.

The Sun will eventually turn into a crystal.
In about 5 billion years, the Sun will exhaust its fuel and shrink into a white dwarf, which will eventually cool and crystallize into a diamond-like structure.

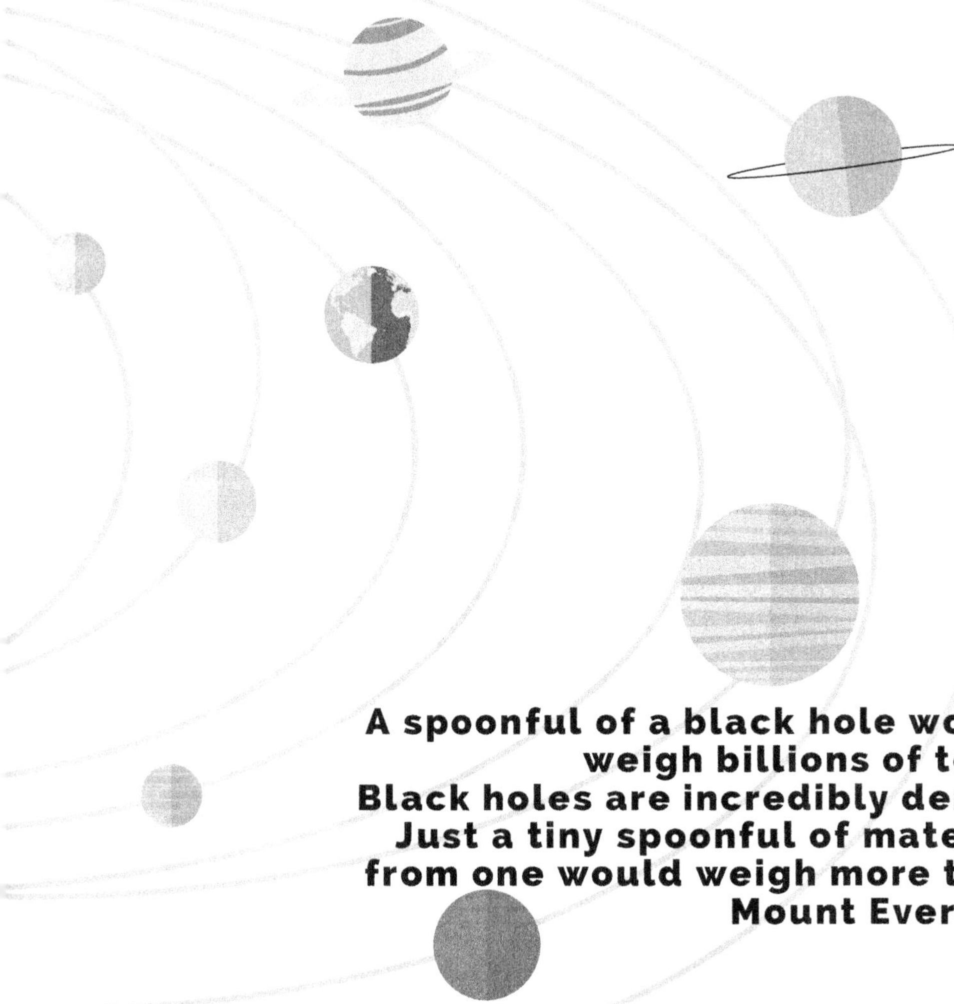

A spoonful of a black hole would weigh billions of tons.
Black holes are incredibly dense. Just a tiny spoonful of material from one would weigh more than Mount Everest!

Moeraki Boulders

Have you heard of the Boulders that were a gift from a god?

The Moeraki Boulders are a set of large, spherical boulders located along Koekohe Beach on the coast of New Zealand. These boulders range in size from just 0.5 meters in diameter to 2.2 meters. What makes the boulders so unusual is their near-perfect spherical shape, although some of them are slightly oval.

It is thought that the boulders formed 60 million years ago, embedded in the cliff face. This occurred through a process called concentration, where minerals accumulated around a core in the sediment over millions of years. It was after the erosion of the surrounding soft cliffs that they were exposed along the beach.

According to Ngai Tahu Maori tradition, the spherical boulders are the remains of food baskets washed ashore from the wreck of the Arai-te-uru canoe, a vital part of Maori mythology. The boulders are a popular tourist attraction, drawing crowds from all over the world; they hold symbolic meaning for local indigenous communities.

The Moeraki Boulders are a blend of natural history, geological wonder, and cultural heritage, making them a must-see feature of New Zealand's coastline.

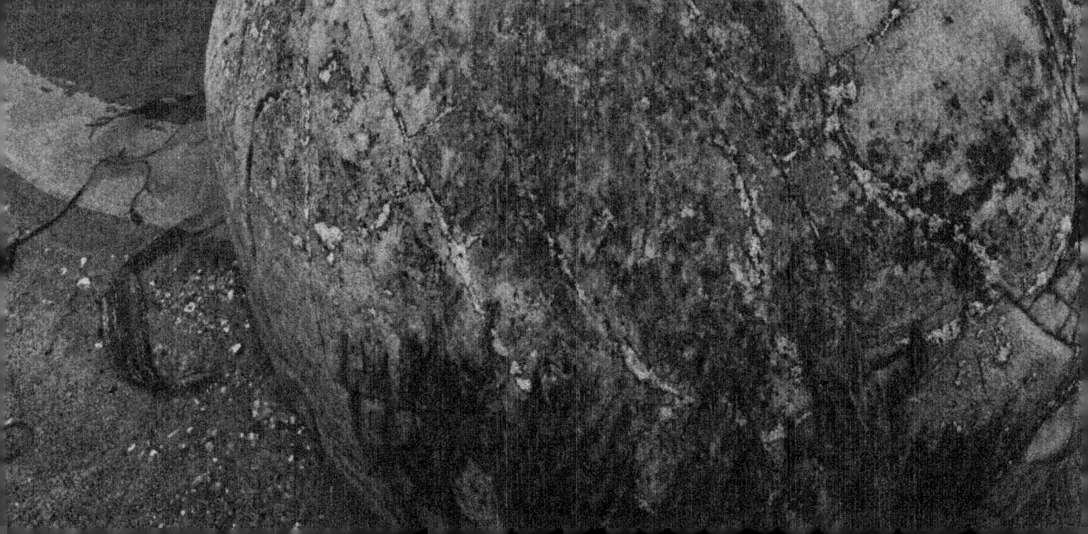

Digestion Details

Why we all fart

As you digest food, your stomach, colon, and intestines fill with gas. The gas is produced when your gut bacteria breaks down food, especially carbohydrates. This needs to be released as a burp or a fart otherwise you can get cramping pains.

Silent but deadly

It's true! The quietest toots are actually the most smelly! Some foods, or digestive processes, cause food to ferment in the intestines. The fermentation creates warm pockets of gas which are full of bacteria. This type of gas moves slowly so it's quiet to emit but the result can create a right old stink! It's usually sulfur that's responsible.

Food culprits

Some foods produce more gas than others. These include spicy foods, acidic foods, red meat, fizzy drinks, high sugar and high fibre foods including beans. Other culprits are Brussels sprouts, cabbage, onions, prunes, and apples.

Fun facts

You can set fire to your fart although this is not recommended. The gasses that make up a fart are mostly flammable.

Toots can move at 10ft per second (3m per second).

The amount of methane in your bottom burp is genetic.

On average, people pass gas 14 times in every 24 hours.

The Devil’s Rope

In 1876, a young man named John Warne Gates staged a dramatic demonstration in San Antonio, Texas. He built a wire fence pen and filled it with what he called ‘The toughest and wildest longhorn cattle in Texas.’

The wire held firm, even when a cowboy charged the cattle, waving flaming brands.

Gates, later known as "Bet-A-Million Gates," was selling barbed wire, a revolutionary fencing material patented by Joseph Glidden of De Kalb, Illinois. Glidden's design, a smooth wire reinforced with twisted barbs, was a game-changer. Gates poetically called it ‘lighter than air, stronger than whiskey, cheaper than dust.’ Farmers, desperate for fencing on the vast, treeless prairie, quickly embraced it.

The 1862 Homestead Act, signed by President Lincoln, offered 160-acre plots to settlers who built homes and worked the land. However, the open plains made property boundaries nearly impossible to maintain. Barbed wire transformed the prairie from an unbounded expanse into manageable farmland.

This transformation wasn’t without conflict. Cowboys detested the wire, as it injured cattle and ended their open-range lifestyle. Native Americans, who had seen their land seized, called it ‘the devil’s rope.’ Fights broke out in the ‘fence-cutting wars,’ with masked gangs destroying fences to reclaim common land. Shootouts and deaths occurred before authorities restored order.

Despite the turmoil, barbed wire flourished. By 1880, Glidden’s factory had produced 263,000 miles of wire, enough to wrap around the globe ten times. Barbed wire reinforced property ownership and transformed the West.

AMERICA'S STONEHENGE

Erected in 1980, these mysterious Guidestones stood tall in Elbert County, Georgia, until 2022. Often referred to as 'America's Stonehenge,' the monument consisted of several upright granite slabs, uniquely arranged in a star pattern, topped by a horizontal capstone. But it wasn't the shape and style of the monument that drew the attention.

The slabs featured inscriptions in eight languages of the modern world. There was also a shorter message in four ancient scripts: Babylonian Cuneiform, Classical Greek, Sanskrit, and Egyptian hieroglyphs. The inscriptions outlined ten principles for humanity:

1. *Maintain humanity under a population of 500 million to maintain a perpetual balance with nature.*
2. *Guide reproduction wisely - to improve fitness and diversity.*
3. *Unite humanity with a living new language for all.*
4. *Rule passion, faith, tradition, and all new things with tempered reason.*
5. *Protect people and nations with fair laws and just courts.*
6. *Let all nations rule internally, resolving external disputes in a worldwide court.*
7. *Avoid petty laws and useless officials.*
8. *Balance personal rights with social duties*
9. *Prize truth, beauty, love, seeking harmony with the infinite.*
10. *Be not a cancer on the Earth - leave room for nature.*

The Elberton Granite Finishing Company built the monument, funded and designed by a private anonymous man, using the pseudonym R.C. Christian who claimed to represent a small group of loyalists concerned about the future of humanity.

Due to the cryptic messages, conspiracy theories grew surrounding the Guidestones. Some people viewed them as a blueprint for a sustainable future, while others interpreted them as evidence of a globalist or occult agenda, citing the population control guideline as particularly controversial.

Unfortunately, in July 2022, vandals set off an explosion near the monument, partially destroying it. Later, the remaining monument had to be taken down because of safety concerns regarding the damaged structure.

Though they are no longer standing, the Georgian Guidestones remain a symbol of speculation and mystery, with their true purpose and the identity of their creators still unknown.

Malpropisms

- Texas has a lot of electrical votes. *(electoral votes)*
- He's a wolf in cheap clothing. *(sheep's clothing)*
- He's the apple of my pie. *(apple of my eye)*
- It's a doggy-dog world out there. *(dog-eat-dog world)*
- Let's nip it in the butt. *(nip it in the bud)*
- We'll burn that bridge when we get to it. *(cross that bridge)*
- He met his nemesis at the chessboard - a worthy component. *(worthy opponent)*

Spoonerisms

- It's roaring with pain *(It's pouring with rain)*
- A lack of pies *(A pack of lies)*
- Belly jeans *(Jelly beans)*
- Wave the sails *(Save the whales)*
- Fight in your race *(Right in your face)*
- Cattle ships and bruisers *(Battleships and cruisers)*
- Know your blows *(Blow your nose)*

Puns

- Don't go bacon my heart!
- I'm not lion when I say you're the best.
- Stop being so catty, just paws and reflect.
- I have a few jokes about chemistry, but I'm afraid they won't get a reaction.
- Reading this book is lit-erary amazing!
- I'd tell you a pizza joke, but it's too cheesy.
- Taco 'bout a party! Let's guac and roll.

The Rubik's Cube was invented in 1974 by Ernő Rubik, a Hungarian architect and professor, as a teaching tool for explaining three-dimensional geometry. It wasn't until he scrambled it and tried to solve it himself that he realized its potential as a puzzle..

The World Cube Association oversees official Rubik's Cube competitions worldwide, where 'speedcubers' compete to solve cubes in record times. The current world record for a single 3x3 solve is an astonishing 3.47 seconds, by Yusheng Du in 2018.

A 3x3 standard Rubik's Cube can be arranged in a staggering 43,252,003,274,489, 856,000 ways. Despite this mind-boggling number, every configuration can be solved in 20 moves or fewer, a fact known as 'God's Number.'

The Rubik's Cube became a global sensation after its international release in 1980. By 1982, over 100 million cubes had been sold, cementing its place as one of the most iconic toys in history..

The smallest functional Rubik's Cube is just 5.6 millimeters wide and can fit on the tip of your finger, while the largest is over 6 feet tall! The classic 3x3 cube isn't the only type—there are easier versions like the 2x2 cube, as well as challenging ones like the 4x4 and 5x5 'Rubik's Revenge.

Solving a Rubik's Cube improves memory, spatial awareness, and problem solving skills. It's also a great way to enhance focus and patience, making it as beneficial as it is entertaining. Ingenious robots can also solve Cube, and the record is an incredible 0.38 seconds.

Incredible Things To Tell Your Friends

Trees use underground fungal networks, often called the 'Wood Wide Web,' to share nutrients and send warning signals to each other.

Rafflesia is the world's largest flower.
Its blooms can grow over 3 feet wide and weigh up to 15 pounds.

Plants can 'hear' sounds.
Studies show some plants respond to vibrations, like those caused by buzzing bees, by increasing nectar production.

The corpse flower smells like rotting flesh.
This rare flower emits a stench to attract pollinators like flies and beetles.

Sequoias are the world's largest trees.
Giant sequoias can grow over 300 feet tall and weigh more than 2.5 million pounds.

The Sensitive Plant reacts to touch.
Mimosa pudica folds its leaves when touched, a defense mechanism to deter predators.

EMU WARS

One of the most bizarre conflicts in history

A war against emus

This unusual showdown unfolded as farmers in Western Australia struggled to protect their wheat crops from an overwhelming invasion of these large, flightless birds. The emu population, booming after their post-migration feast, wreaked havoc on the already strained farms.

Desperate for help, the farmers turned to the Australian government, whose solution was as extraordinary as the problem itself: send in the military. Under the command of Major G.P.W. Meredith, soldiers armed with ammunition launched a campaign to cull the emus. What followed was nothing short of surreal.

After weeks of failed efforts and mounting embarrassment, the government withdrew its forces, leaving the emus victorious in what became known as the "Great Emu War." News of the military's defeat spread quickly, sparking ridicule worldwide.

New Word Entries in the Oxford English Dictionary

Bizzo: An object where the exact name cannot be remembered.
Bloss: A person who looks ridiculous or scruffy.
Blunnies: Ankle high strong leather with elastic boots.
Breakfasty: Similar to breakfast.
Brokeness: Having little or no money.
Catnap: To steal a cat and keep it as your own pet.
Coolite: An inexpensive, lightweight surfboard.
Dead air: Unintentional period of silence.
Dead dog: A lost cause.
Dillbrain: A silly person.
Doco: Doumentary TV programme.
Dooligah: Large, hairy, foul-smelling creature
Fatmouth: Make empty threats.
Foot falcon: Walking swiftly.
Katsu: Japanese curry.

Kintsugi: To mend pottery by filling cracks with lacquer dusted with powdered gold.
Rooned: To express pessimism about the future.
Seva: Selfless service to other people.
Stot: To bounce or rebound from a surface.
Tidda: A woman of your own generation.
Viennoiserie: Baked goods made with pastry or dough that has been enriched with butter.

The Money Pit
on Oak Island

In 1795, on a small island in Nova Scotia, Daniel McGinnis and his friends noticed something unusual. Some interesting signs and a depression in the ground made them curious.

Daniel and his friends started digging out the depression, and what they found was unexpected. Every 10 feet (3 meters), they found layers of logs, which suggested there was a man-made shaft. However, they needed more digging power, so the Onslow company became involved.

As they dug further, the mystery literally deepened. They found layers of charcoal, putty, and coconut fiber, which was not native to the island. Could this suggest a hidden, buried treasure? But when the shaft got to 90ft deep, the real mystery was found. There was a stone tablet with indecipherable inscriptions, which some people thought was a warning of traps.

Not long after this, seawater flooded the shaft stopping any further digging. They did not understand why this happened and had to pause the dig. With the development of technology, they realized that the series of tunnels led to nearby Smith’s Cove, which was the seawater's source. Some people believe this flooding of the tunnel was one of the booby traps mentioned on the stone tablet.

Many people and numerous companies have attempted to solve the mystery over the years. Excavations have uncovered artifacts like tools, coins, and wood but no conclusive treasure.

The flooding and booby traps together have made the excavation of the pit famously difficult and costly, and without any treasure in sight, excavation has ceased, and the money pit remains a mystery.

SLANG SAFARI

- [ ] Fat Cat
- [ ] Lone Wolf
- [ ] Dirty Dog
- [ ] Big Bear
- [ ] Monkey Business
- [ ] Cool Cat
- [ ] Bird Brain
- [ ] Antsy
- [ ] Grasshopper
- [ ] Cool Crocodile
- [ ] Chameleon
- [ ] Frog in your Throat
- [ ] Top Dog
- [ ] Moth to a Flame
- [ ] Social Butterfly
- [ ] Queen Bee
- [ ] Early Bird
- [ ] Fishy
- [ ] Copycat
- [ ] Fly on the Wall
- [ ] Shark
- [ ] Underdog
- [ ] Wolf in Sheep's Clothing
- [ ] Hornet's Nest
- [ ] Snake Charmer
- [ ] Sitting Duck
- [ ] Crocodile Tears
- [ ] Bugged Out
- [ ] Wise Owl
- [ ] Fish out of Water

FASCINATING!!

Dolphins are known for their remarkable intelligence and social behavior, including their ability to protect humans from sharks. There are numerous documented cases where dolphins have formed protective circles around swimmers in danger, blocking sharks from getting too close. This behavior is believed to stem from their strong group instincts and natural tendency to defend against predators. Dolphins use their agility, speed, and even their powerful snouts to nudge or ram sharks, often deterring them completely.

In the 1879, Williamina Flemming was hired as a maid for the Pickerings, a couple that ran the Harvard Observatory. Mrs Pickering persuaded her husband to employ the maid at the observatory after she recognized Williamina's intelligence. The former maid ended up classifying over 10,000 stars and being nominated for the Bruce medal.

The heart of a blue whale is so large that a human could swim through its arteries.

In 1991, researchers at the University of Cambridge's Computer Lab were tired of making trips to the break room only to find the coffee pot empty. To solve this, they set up a camera aimed at the coffee machine and connected it to their computer network, allowing everyone to check the coffee level remotely. This small invention became the world's first webcam

NAMES PEOPLE USE

for Diarrhea

Never Ask The General Public

(when voting contests go wrong)

In 2012, Walmart launched a Facebook Poll to agree the location for a Pitbull concert at one of their stores. Two comedians, David Thorpe and Jon Hendren, persuaded their following to vote for the most remote Walmart and the site duely won the poll. Pitbull accepted the result and invited the comedians to join him on his trip to Kodiak, Alaska and one of them even went along.

William Shatner, of Star Trek fame, tried to get two of Pluto's moons named Romulus and Vulcan, both mythical planets from the tv show. Romulus was rejected as it was already in use but Vulcan won the poll. However SETI failed to honor the vote and picked their own favorite names instead.

A computer science graduate, Roland Bunce, almost won a 'Make Me A Model' competition where the prize included a meeting with the modeling agency, Storm. Pranksters made a Facebook fan page to get him 66,000 votes before Roland decided to withdraw himself from the competition.

Vegemite ran a poll to name their new product which consisted of Vegemite mixed with cream cheese. The winner was iSnack 2.0 and Vegemite went along with the new name, selling 3 million jars, before rebranding as Cheesybite.

In 1998, 'Hank the Angry Dwarf' won People magazine's poll for the most beautiful person on the earth. He beat Leonado DiCaprio and Madonna.

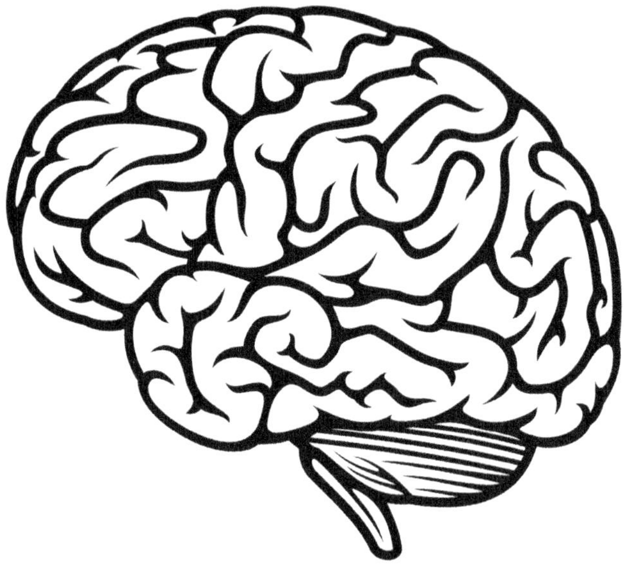

Bizarre Brain facts

The Brain Has No Pain Receptors

The brain itself doesn't feel pain, which is why brain surgeries can be performed on awake patients. The pain you feel from headaches comes from surrounding tissues, not the brain.

Your Brain Creates Its Own Reality

Your brain fills in gaps in your vision. The blind spot in your eye doesn't register because your brain makes up what it 'thinks' should be there.

The Brain Works Harder When You're Asleep

During REM sleep, your brain is highly active, consolidating memories and processing information from the day. It's more productive than when you're awake!

THE MOST OUTRAGOUS
AMUSEMENT PARK

In Vernon, New Jersey, Action Park earned a reputation not just as an amusement park but as a battleground for thrill-seekers willing to risk life and limb. Gene Mulvihill opened the park in 1978. The park's 'maximum freedom' philosophy resulted in notoriously unsafe rides, minimal risk assessment, and countless injuries. By the time it closed in 1996, it had become known as 'Class Action Park.'

Action Park featured rides so dangerous that they sound unreal. The Cannonball Loop, a water slide with a full vertical loop, caused injuries ranging from nosebleeds to stuck riders. The Alpine Slide—a concrete track where guests raced down on flimsy sleds—was responsible for broken bones and burns. The Wave Pool, dubbed "The Grave Pool," was so intense that lifeguards rescued up to 30 people daily. Other infamous rides included the Tarzan Swing, where guests frequently struggled with icy water shocks, and Motorworld's Speedboats, where guests often crashed into barriers or each other.

Action Park wasn't just dangerous because of the rides; its culture made it a breeding ground for disaster. The staff, often teenagers with minimal training, struggled to enforce rules. Alcohol flowed freely at the park, exacerbating guests' recklessness. As guests signed liability waivers upon entering, many injuries and incidents went unreported.

Gene Mulvihill's approach to the park was equally reckless. He frequently ignored safety concerns, reportedly bribed inspectors, and carried no liability insurance, instead self-insuring under a dubious legal loophole.

Despite its grim history, Action Park remains a symbol of wild independence. Today, the site operates as Mountain Creek Waterpark under far stricter safety standards. Yet, the legend of Action Park lives on—a relic of an era where danger was part of the thrill.

Wonderful Words

Snollygoster – A shrewd, unprincipled person, especially a politician.

Eucatastrophe – A sudden and favorable resolution of events in a story.

Limerence – The state of being infatuated or obsessed with another person.

Pandiculation – The act of stretching and yawning, especially on waking.

Blatherskite – Someone who talks a lot without making much sense.

Flibbertigibbet – A frivolous, flighty, or excessively talkative person.

Mugwump – A person who remains independent, especially from politics.

Bumbershoot – An old-fashioned term for an umbrella.

Catawampus – Askew or not lined up correctly.

Brouhaha – A noisy and overexcited reaction or response.

Bibble – To eat or drink noisily.

Futz – To waste time or busy oneself with unimportant matters.

Whirligig – A spinning toy or something that whirls.

Gongoozler – Someone who enjoys watching canal or waterway activities.

Flapdoodle – Nonsense or foolish talk.

Gewgaw – A showy but worthless trinket.

Underground Treasure

Deep beneath the bustling streets of London lies one of the most secure and mysterious places in the world: the Bank of England's gold vault. This underground fortress is home to nearly 400,000 gold bars, worth a jaw-dropping £200 billion. Built in 1694, the Bank's vault is so massive and famous that it rivals Fort Knox in the U.S.

The vault is a fortress in every sense, designed to withstand everything from natural disasters to potential attacks. With walls several feet thick and doors that weigh tons, it's nearly impenetrable. Even getting inside requires layers of top-secret security, including voice recognition, codes, and keys.

But one of the vault's most legendary stories comes from a surprise discovery in 1836. A Victorian sewer worker found an unexpected path into the vault. While repairing a drain, he stumbled across an old underground passageway that led directly beneath the gold vault. Instead of helping himself to some gold bars, he decided to alert the Bank of England.

To prove his point, he sent anonymous letters to the Bank's directors, claiming he could access the vault. They didn't believe him at first but eventually agreed to meet him inside the vault at a specific time. Sure enough, at the agreed hour, a noise came from the floor—and the man popped up through the floorboards!

Luckily, a stock check revealed he hadn't taken anything. Impressed by his honesty, the Bank rewarded him with £800, equivalent to about £80,000 today.

The vault remains a crucial part of the global economy and a symbol of incredible security. And who knows—maybe it's still hiding a few more secrets deep underground!

THE MYSTERY OF THE AIRPLANE HIJACKER

On November 24, 1971, a man calling himself Dan Cooper boarded Northwest Orient Airlines Flight 305 from Washington to Seattle-Tacoma International Airport. He was calm and well-dressed in a suit and tie and did not raise any alarms with the crew.

The plane was mid-flight when Dan handed a member of the cabin crew a note, which she promptly put in her pocket dismissing it as flirtatious behavior, until Mr Cooper said: "Miss, you better look at that note, I have a bomb."

Cooper showed the flight attendant a briefcase containing wires, red sticks, and a battery. He then dictated his demands:

- $200,000 in unmarked $20 bills.
- Four parachutes (two primary and two reserves)
- A fuel truck standing by in Seattle to refuel the plane.

The crew onboard complied with Cooper's demands, landing smoothly in Seattle. Once on the ground, Cooper received the ransom money and parachutes. He allowed the 36 passengers and two flight attendants to disembark but kept the pilot, co-pilot, one flight attendant, and the flight engineer on board.

Once the plane had been refueled, Cooper instructed the crew to fly towards Mexico, keeping the plane at a low altitude and slow speed. He also demanded that the cabin remain unpressurized and the rear staircase remained deployed.

At roughly 8 pm, Cooper donned one of the parachutes, and holding the ransom money in a knapsack, jumped out the rear door of the plane.

They were somewhere over southwestern Washington, with nothing but rugged terrain underneath them. The weather conditions were poor, with heavy rain, strong winds, and freezing temperatures, making the jump difficult for even an experienced skydiver.

Cooper was never seen again.

However, in 1980, a young boy digging on the banks of the Columbia River near Vancouver, Washington, discovered $5,800 in deteriorated $20 bills matching the serial numbers of Cooper's ransom money.

Further searches of the area uncovered other pieces of evidence, including a clip-on black tie and some cigarette butts smoked by Cooper (that the FBI later lost), none of which could provide enough DNA to yield a match.

There are many theories about what happened to Dan Cooper, but in 2016, the FBI officially closed the case, citing a lack of viable leads and needing to allocate resources elsewhere.

What do you think happened to Mr Cooper?

Some people think that he died in the jump whilst others think he survived and lived out his life under a new identity.

★ Funky Feet Facts ★

Toe wrestling is a competitive sport.

Feet get bigger throughout the day.

A quarter of all of the bones in the human body are in the feet.

Your feet can produce up to one cup of sweat per day.

Big toes used to be able to manoeuvre in the same way as thumbs.

Some people have more than 5 toes on their foot.

Toe cheese is made up of lint, bacteria, dead skin, and fungi.

Feet are the most ticklish part of the body.

Museum Marvels

Toilet Seat Art Museum

In San Antonio, Texas, there's a captivating museum called the Toilet Seat Art Museum. Founded by Barney Smith, a retired plumber, and passionate artist, this museum is dedicated to artistic works made on or featuring toilet seats. It showcases over 1,400 decorated toilet seats, each transformed into a canvas for Smith's creativity. The themes range from historical events to pop culture and personal milestones. Smith began his toilet seat hobby as a fun way to merge his plumbing skills with his artistic interests. Initially, the museum started in Smith's garage but has recently relocated to Truck Yard, a Dallas venue where it continues to delight visitors.

A Chicken Who Needs Glasses

There is a small unknown museum in London that is stocked to the brim with spectacles. Famous spectacles in the collection are ones worn by legendary TV star Ronnie Corbett and Dr. Johnson. They even have a set of contact lenses that were worn by Matt LeBlanc during his time on Friends! However, a chicken in the corner is one of the strangest items in the collection. The chicken wears a pair of opaque red shades perched upon its beak; this is to prevent it from seeing rival roosters and turning aggressive.

The Cursed Diamond

Natural History Museum of the Smithsonian Institution in Washington, D.C. is home to the Hope Diamond. Weighing 45.52 carats, the large blue diamond is worth around $250 million. However, it is said to be stolen from a Hindu god's statue who placed a curse upon the gem. Some owners of the diamond have experienced unfortunate accidents and personal tragedies. Under exposure to UV light, the diamond glows with a red phosphorescence, which may also have contributed to its reputation of being cursed.

SO MUCH FUN

The human body emits a faint bioluminescent glow, but it's 1,000 times weaker than the naked eye can detect.

The first mechanical alarm clock, invented in 1787, was fixed to ring at one time only - 4 a.m.

Sloths move so slowly that algae grows on them. This gives them a greenish tint, which acts as camouflage in trees.

In 1989, Pepsi traded soda for a fleet of Soviet military equipment, including 17 submarines, briefly making it a naval power.

When threatened, sea cucumbers eject their internal organs to distract predators and then regenerate them.

You can't hum while holding your nose. Without airflow through your nose, it's impossible to hum.

There's a Rainbow Eucalyptus Tree: Its bark peels off in layers, revealing vibrant rainbow colors underneath.

The word 'Robot' comes from a play where it referred to artificial workers

The world's very first website, created by Sir Tim Berners-Lee in 1991, is still online and accessible at https://info.cern.ch/hypertext/WWW/TheProject.html.

10 SURVIVAL MYTHS

1. **In a falling elevator, jump before it gets to the bottom.** Jumping would have little effect on the speed of your fall. Luckily, elevators are incredibly safe.
2. **You need to ration water until you are rescued.** Preventing water loss through perspiration and digestion is more important.
3. **You can shelter from a tornado under a highway bridge.** Wind will funnel under a bridge, accelerate, and bring debris. It's safer to stay in your car or lie in a ditch.
4. **You can survive in the desert by drinking cactus water.** Cactus water contains toxic acids and alkaloids and should not be drunk. Only juice from prickly pears is safe to drink.
5. **Suck the poison out of a snakebite wound.** Putting your mouth on the bite can lead to infection. Cutting open the wound is not advised either, as it can damage nerves.
6. **You can drink your own urine to survive.** Urine is a waste product and won't rehydrate you. However, soaking your clothes in urine to keep yourself cool and prevent water loss from sweating is a good idea.
7. **To get away from a bear, run downhill.** Bears can run in any direction at speeds of up to 30mph. They are best avoided.
8. **If attacked, punch a shark on the nose.** The nose is too close to the mouth, and you don't want your hands in there. Instead, go for the eyes or gills.
9. **If you get stabbed, pull the object out of you.** The implement effectively 'plugs the hole' and reduces bleeding. Instead, apply pressure to the wound and get help.
10. **If you run in a zigzag, an alligator won't catch you.** Running in straight line is much faster!

SURPRISING!!

In 2012, a U.S. company discovered that their systems were being accessed from China. At first, it seemed like a sophisticated hack, but the culprit turned out to be "Bob," a quiet, unassuming employee in his 40s. Bob had outsourced his programming work to a firm in China, even mailing them his security credentials. While his Chinese contractors worked hard, Bob spent his days surfing Reddit, watching cat videos, and shopping online. He paid them a fraction of his six-figure salary and earned glowing performance reviews for years. However, when his secret was uncovered, Bob was promptly fired.

The very first text message ever sent was "Merry Christmas"! It was sent on December 3, 1992, by Neil Papworth to Richard Jarvis. Neil used the Vodafone GSM network in the UK to send it, marking the start of texting as we know it today.

Koalas have fingerprints so similar to humans' that they can confuse crime scene investigators.

A 2009 Burger King marketing campaign encouraged people to delete 10 Facebook friends in exchange for a free Whopper. Once friends were removed, they'd get a notification saying they had been 'sacrificed for a Whopper.' The bold idea gained massive attention but also sparked controversy, leading Facebook to shut it down after just 10 days, citing privacy concerns.

RULES FOR ROYALS

The British Royal Family lives by a few unusual rules

1

No Garlic

There are a bunch of foods that the royal family is not allowed to have because of the danger that comes with eating them, but that's not the case with garlic. Instead, the ban on garlic is simply because the past Queen disliked it so much. A former royal chef, Darren McGrady, told reporters, "We can never serve anything with garlic or too much onion," and "We also couldn't serve meat that was rare, as she liked her meat more well done." It's not yet reported if the new King Charles has lifted the garlic ban or if he has introduced other food bans during his reign.

2

Tiaras

There are very strict rules regarding what the royals can and cannot wear. One of these examples is all about hats. The royals are known for their outrageous hats and tiaras, but do you know when they're should wear them? Hats should be worn until 6pm, and then they changed to tiaras at public events.

But why?

It is an age-old tradition that is used for married women to show a sign of their status and to indicate that they are taken and not looking for a husband.

3

Pack Black

This is one of the most morbid rules that the royal family has. The rule is that when the royal family travels, no matter where they go, each family member must pack an all-black outfit. This rule was put in place after Queen Elizabeth II landed back in the UK following her father's death and had to wait on the plane until an appropriate mourning outfit was brought onboard for her to change into. This moment was to be one of the most photographed moments of Elizabeth's life, and so the appropriate mourning outfit was incredibly important.

4

Travel Plans

The rule is that two or more heirs to the throne must not travel together. This means they may not share a car or a plane. This protects the line of succession and ensures the royal family's legacy is secure. However, this rule was already broken back in 2014 when Prince William took his then-infant son, Prince George, on a trip with him and his wife, Princess Katherine, to Australia and New Zealand.

5

No Touching

When people meet a member of the royal family for the first time, they are briefed on expected behavior. Guests should bow or curtsey, not intrude on personal space, and not touch the Royals at any point. Though not every royal family member accepts or acts on this rule, it is mainly reserved for public formal occasions. Anyone touching a Royal usually creates quite a stir on social media and among those familiar with this royal protocol.

Fun Findings

On the planet Jupiter, it rains down diamonds.

Cotton candy (candy floss) was actually invented by a dentist.

Hot water freezes faster than cold water.

Rhubarb grows so quickly that you can hear the plant squeaking as the stalks get larger.

Crows can be trained to recognize human faces.

In the 1982 movie, ET, the sound effect for ET's footsteps was created by squeezing jelly wrapped in a wet towel.

AMAZING ANIMALS

The Basilisk Lizard, found in Central and South America is known as the 'Jesus Christ Lizard,' because it can run across water for up to 15 feet.
Its long toes and lightweight body create air pockets that keep it from sinking, a miraculous adaptation for escaping predators.

In Central Africa, the hairy frog amphibian, also known as the "Wolverine Frog," breaks its own bones to produce sharp claws that protrude through its skin when threatened. It's a gruesome yet effective defense mechanism against predators.

The Arctic Tern has the longest migration of any animal, flying around 44,000 miles annually between its Arctic breeding grounds and the Antarctic, where it enjoys endless summer. Over its lifetime, it can travel the equivalent of three trips to the moon and back.

In Australia, the inland taipan, often called the "fierce snake," holds the title of the most venomous snake on Earth, with venom capable of killing 100 adult humans in a single bite, though it rarely encounters people.

Known as the "walking fish," the axolotl, found in the lakes of Mexico, is a salamander that never grows out of its juvenile stage, maintaining its gills and aquatic lifestyle for life. Remarkably, it can regenerate entire limbs, spinal cords, and even parts of its brain.

Yukky Things To Tell Your Friends

Earwax is a natural cleaning agent.
It traps dirt and dust to protect your ears, and it's made of dead skin cells, oil, and sweat.

Your stomach replaces Its lining every few days.
This protects it from being digested by its own acid.

Your tongue is as unique as your fingerprint.
No two tongues have the same print, making it a fantastic, but under used, identifier.

During your lifetime, you produce enough saliva to fill two swimming pools.
as the average person produces about 25,000 quarts of saliva in total.

Your belly button is a bacterial jungle.
Studies have found over 2,000 species of bacteria in human belly buttons, with some species unique to individuals.

You shed about 40 pounds of skin in your lifetime.
Dead skin cells are continuously replaced, contributing to the dust in your home.

THE MOVING ROCKS

In Racetrack Playa, a dry lakebed in Death Valley National Park, California, there's a natural phenomenon of moving rocks.

Large stones, some weighing hundreds of pounds, appear to move across the dry, flat surface of the playa, leaving long, shallow tracks behind them in the mud. Despite no apparent external forces moving the rocks, the trails can stretch for hundreds of feet in straight, curved, or zigzag patterns.

Due to the mysterious nature of the movements, some speculate paranormal forces or alien involvement. Others propose that high winds pushed the rocks across the surface, though the size and weight of the stones challenge this. Another theory suggests that ice sheets could form around the rocks, making it easier for the wind to slide them across the basin of the playa.

However, sadly, the reality is not as exciting. In 2014, researchers Richard Norris and James Norris used GPS trackers and time-lapse photography to solve this fascinating mystery. What happens is that during the rare rains in the Baisin, water accumulates on the playa around the stones, creating slippery mud. Overnight, as the temperature drops, a thin layer of ice forms. As the sun then rises, the ice thaws and becomes slippy; although the rock movement is nearly imperceptible to the naked eye, the rocks leave tell-tale trails.

This makes these moving rocks a unique geological mystery that showcases the interplay of natural forces. They are a popular subject for scientific study and have also become a tourist attraction, although visitors are urged to respect the fragile environment.

BIZARRE EVENTS

On March 13, 1997, in Phoenix, Arizona, one of the most widely reported and debated UFO incidents in modern history occurred.

Between the hours of 8:30pm and 9pm, witnesses across Arizona, Nevada, Sonora, and Mexico reported seeing massive, V-shaped formations of lights silently moving across the sky. The lights in the sky were described as having a red-orange color and an orb-like shape. The lights were attached to a single large object or multiple smaller crafts.

Later that same evening, around 10 pm, another set of lights appeared stationary near Phoenix, hovering in the sky before gradually disappearing. Descriptions varied, with some claiming to see a solid, massive craft, while others reported a formation of independent lights.

Many witnesses saw the lights, including residents, pilots, law enforcement officers, and even the Governor of Arizona, Fife Symington, who witnessed the phenomenon. But what was the cause of these mysterious lights?

Many believed the lights were from an alien spacecraft due to their silence, huge size, and synchronized movement. Some people believe the U.S. Air Force attributed the stationary lights to flares dropped during a training exercise at the Barry Goldwater Range near Phoenix. Skeptics suggest the V-shaped lights were aircraft flying in formation.

The Phoenix Lights remain a famous case in UFO lore, inspiring documentaries, books, and films. While many accept the military's explanation, others view the event as one of the most credible UFO sightings in history because of the number of witnesses and the vivid descriptions.

Fruity Facts

Strawberries are not berries!

Generally speaking, people commonly name berry any fruit that is small, pulpy, juicy, looks somewhat round, and doesn't have a stone. However, the botanical definition of berry is a lot more exclusive, as it refers to any fruit produced from the ovary of a single flower. Using this definition, strawberries are not berries. This is because a strawberry is made of multiple tiny fruits called achenes—the little seed-like spots you see on the flesh.

Bananas are clones!

Bananas can't be grown from seeds, making them technically "sterile." Instead, they are propagated by taking a piece of an existing banana plant and growing it—essentially cloning the original plant.

Apples are full of air!

Apples are 25% air which is why they are perfect for apple bobbing at Halloween. It also means apples can be stored in quantities without being crushed under their own weight.

Figs are dependent on wasps!

Tiny fig wasps are vital for the pollination of figs. They burrow into small openings and lay eggs inside the figs. At the same time, the little wasp deposits pollen that they have picked up whilst outside the fig. As the openings are tiny, the wasp loses its wings as they enter the fig. However, an enzyme in the fig breaks down the dead wasps, and they are absorbed back into the fruit, so no one eats dead wasps.

Bananas are radioactive!

Bananas are technically radioactive due to their high levels of the isotope potassium-40. The good news? They're completely safe unless you consume around 700 bananas every day for your entire life!

Grapes can explode!

There is so much water in a grape that putting it into a microwave can cause the grape to explode.

The Fart Poem

A fart can be delightful, it's like a bottom sneeze,
It warms the bed in Winter and kills off all the fleas.
Sometimes a fart is quiet, but often, it is loud,
And turns the air around into a smelly cloud.
A short bottom burp or something rather long
Can sometimes be likened to a favorite song.
The explosive noise sounds just like a medley
But the accompanying smell can be quite deadly.
Colorless, odorless, sometimes rather vile,
Some are barely noticed, others linger a while.
Uncontrollable farts appear in lots of places
Leaving their owners with red, embarrassed faces.
From open air festivals to a tiny elevator,
A fart can just appear like a sneaky traitor.
If you feel one coming, don't follow through
Or else the one embarrassed is going to be you!

Startup Squatter

Eric Simons, a 19-year-old entrepreneur from Chicago, turned a bold idea into reality in one of the most unexpected ways: by secretly living on AOL's Palo Alto campus for two months.

Simons had been part of AOL's K12 incubator program, which helped young entrepreneurs develop their ideas. When the program ended, he noticed his office badge still worked. Instead of packing up and leaving, Eric decided to stay.

Staying undetected in a busy tech headquarters wasn't easy, but Eric found clever ways to blend in:

- Working Late: Eric stayed in the office after hours, making it look like he was just putting in extra effort. He worked on his startup until the building was almost empty, waiting for the security patrols to die down.
- Sleeping Spots: He found couches just outside the security guards' usual rounds and made them his makeshift beds.
- Morning Gym Routine: To avoid suspicion, Eric hit the office gym early in the morning before employees arrived. This routine kept him clean and refreshed and boosted his fitness.
- Living on a Budget: Simons kept his expenses shockingly low, spending just $30 in his first month. He relied on free office snacks and found creative ways to stretch his resources.

After two months, a guard caught him sleeping and kicked him out. Although his stint came to an end, Eric's audacious story became the talk of the tech world.

AOL's Response

Instead of being furious, AOL had a surprisingly lighthearted reaction. David Temkin, AOL's senior vice president, said, 'It was always our intention to support entrepreneurship—we just didn't expect it to work so well.'

DID YOU KNOW?

A real bear inspired Winnie the Pooh

Did you know there was a real bear that inspired Christopher Robin's Winnie-the-Pooh? There was a lovely black bear named Winnie (short for Winnipeg) who lived at the London Zoo. Christopher Robin often visited the Zoo as a child, and it was noticed that he had a particular inclination for Winnie. This isn't the only thing within the books that's inspired by reality. Winnie-the-Pooh's insatiable love for honey is also shared by wild bears as a source of energy.

DID YOU KNOW?

Bears can be actors

Well, at least one could. Gentle Ben was played by a real-life grizzly bear named Bruno in the 1967 TV series of the same title. The series goes on to depict Ben as a friendly bear who bonds with a boy named Mark. Together they share a love for nature and wildlife. Bruno was bred and raised in captivity, which is why he was known for his calm, predictable behavior. It was also why he was able to learn and follow commands. After his few years of fame on TV, Bruno retired to a wildlife sanctuary.

The Meguro Parasitological Museum in Japan can tell you everything you ever wanted to find out about parasites including parasitic crabs and head lice.
The museum was founded by a medical doctor who was conducting research.
Exhibits include a gross 25ft (8m) long tape worm.

In Leeds Castle, Kent, England, you can find a museum dedicated to dog collars.
The oldest collar dates from the 15th century and was probably worn to protect the dog's neck from wolves and bears.
Some collars are designed to display wealth and are made from silver whilst others are made from beads or old tyres.

Kansas has an entire museum dedicated to barbed wire.
It has over 2,000 different patterns of barbed wire on display.
Visitors are encouraged to look but not to touch!

The Museum of Medieval Torture Instruments can be found in Amsterdam.
It has over 100 torture devices on display in dimly lit rooms.
Well known items including a guillotine and thumb screws are on display as well as an iron maiden, Scold's bridle and Catherine wheels.
Some devices are original whilst others are reproduction.

Portland, Maine houses the International Cryptozoology Museum which covers the study of animals whose existance is not yet confirmed such as the Yeti and the Loch Ness Monster.
Exhibits include evidence of these animals and artwork of what the animals are thought to look like.
Evidence of 'existance' includes Sasquatch poop and plaster casts of footprints.

Weird Museums

AMAZING!

Other books by Alex Smart

Trivia book by Alex Smart for kids aged 8-88

<u>About the author</u>

"I love giving people fun gifts that make them laugh! "

Alex Smart is the best-selling author of puzzle and trivia books, including the Things To Do While You Poo series.

After spending one December in a panic-buying frenzy, she created her books to be high-quality, yet inexpensive, gifts for all those 'hard-to-buy-for' people in her life.

Alex has always loved organizing quizzes and hosting silly 'game nights' for friends and family. She is fascinated by quirky trivia and loves unusual, jaw-dropping facts.

She and her husband live in Devon, England, where they can enjoy a relaxing puzzle book whilst exploring the country by train. Occasionally, she enjoys being locked in a room with her adult children and trying to escape in under an hour.

★ ★ ★ ★ ★

Thank you for buying this book, and I hope that you enjoyed all the puzzles.

If you can leave a review on Amazon, I would greatly appreciate it.

If you wish to contact me, my email is
alex@alexsmartbooks.com

Printed in Dunstable, United Kingdom

80957408R00057